Thoughtful Machine Learning

Matthew Kirk

Beijing · Cambridge · Farnham · Köln · Sebastopol · Tokyo

Thoughtful Machine Learning

by Matthew Kirk

Printed in the United States of America.

Published by O'Reilly Media, Inc., 1005 Gravenstein Highway North, Sebastopol, CA 95472.

O'Reilly books may be purchased for educational, business, or sales promotional use. Online editions are also available for most titles (*http://safaribooksonline.com*). For more information, contact our corporate/institutional sales department: 800-998-9938 or *corporate@oreilly.com* .

Editors: Mike Loukides and Ann Spencer
Production Editor: Melanie Yarbrough
Copyeditor: Rachel Monaghan
Proofreader: Jasmine Kwityn

Indexer: Ellen Troutman-Zaig
Interior Designer: David Futato
Cover Designer: Ellie Volkhausen
Illustrator: Rebecca Demarest

October 2014:   First Edition

Revision History for the First Edition
2014-09-23:   First Release
2015-01-16:   Second Release

See *http://oreilly.com/catalog/errata.csp?isbn=9781449374068* for release details.

978-1-449-37406-8

[LSI]

Table of Contents

Preface

This book is about approaching tough problems. Machine learning is an amazing application of computation because it tackles problems that are straight out of science fiction. These algorithms can solve voice recognition, mapping, recommendations, and disease detection. The applications are endless, which is what makes machine learning so fascinating.

This flexibility is also what makes machine learning daunting. It can solve many problems, but how do we know whether we're solving the right problem, or actually solving it in the first place? On top of that sadly much of academic coding standards are lax.

Up until this moment there hasn't been a lot of talk about writing good quality code when it comes to machine learning and that is unfortunate. The ability for us to disseminate an idea across an entire industry is based on our ability to communicate it effectively. And if we write bad code, it's doubtful a lot of people will listen.

Writing this book is my answer to that problem. Teaching machine learning to people in an easier to approach way. This subject is tough, and it's compounded by hard to read code, or ancient C implementations that make zero sense.

While a lot of people will be confused as to why this book is written in Ruby instead of Python, it's because writing tests in Ruby is a beautiful way of explaining your code. The entire book taking this test driven approach is about communication, and communicating the beautiful world of Machine Learning.

What to Expect from This Book

This book is not an exhaustive machine learning resource. For that I'd highly recommend Peter Flach's *Machine Learning: The Art and Science of Algorithms that Make Sense of Data* (Cambridge University Press) or if you are mathematically inclined, Tom Mitchell's Machine Learning series is top notch. There are also great tidbits from

Artificial Intelligence: A Modern Approach, Third Edition by Stuart Russell and Peter Norvig (Prentice Hall).

After reading this book you will not have a PhD in machine learning, but I hope to give you enough information to get working on real problems using data with machine learning. You should expect lots of examples of the approach to problems as well as how to use them at a fundamental level.

You should also find yourself learning how to approach problems that are more fuzzy than the normal unit testing scenario.

How to Read This Book

The best way to read this book is to find examples that excite you. Each chapter aims to be fairly contained, although at times they won't be. My goal for this book is not to be purely theoretical but to introduce you to some examples of problems that machine learning can solve for you as well as some worked out samples of how I'd approach working with data.

In most of the chapters, I try to introduce some business cases in the beginning then delve into a worked out example toward the end. This book is intended as a short read because I want you to focus on working with the code and thinking about these problems instead of getting steeped up in theory.

Who This Book Is For

There are three main people I have written the book for: the developer, the CTO, and the business analyst.

The developer already knows how to write code and is interested in learning more about the exciting world of machine learning. She has some background in working out problems in a computational context and may or may not write Ruby. The book is primarily focused on this persona but there is also the CTO and the business analyst.

The CTO is someone who really wants to know how to utilize machine learning to improve his company. He might have heard of K-Means, K-Nearest Neighbors but hasn't quite figured out how it's applicable to him. The business analyst is similar except that she is less technically inclined. These two personas I wrote the start of every chapter for.

How to Contact Me

I love receiving emails from people who either liked a presentation I gave or need help with a problem. Feel free to email me at *matt@matthewkirk.com*. And to cement this, I will gladly buy you a cup of coffee if you come to the Seattle area (and our schedules permit).

If you'd like to view any of the code in this book, it's free at GitHub (*http://github.com/ thoughtfulml*).

Conventions Used in This Book

The following typographical conventions are used in this book:

Italic
Indicates new terms, URLs, email addresses, filenames, and file extensions.

`Constant width`
Used for program listings, as well as within paragraphs to refer to program elements such as variable or function names, databases, data types, environment variables, statements, and keywords.

`Constant width bold`
Shows commands or other text that should be typed literally by the user.

`Constant width italic`
Shows text that should be replaced with user-supplied values or by values determined by context.

 This element signifies a tip or suggestion.

 This element signifies a general note.

 This element indicates a warning or caution.

 This element indicates a warning of significant importance; read carefully.

Using Code Examples

Supplemental material (code examples, exercises, etc.) is available for download at *http://github.com/thoughtfulml*.

This book is here to help you get your job done. In general, if example code is offered with this book, you may use it in your programs and documentation. You do not need to contact us for permission unless you're reproducing a significant portion of the code. For example, writing a program that uses several chunks of code from this book does not require permission. Selling or distributing a CD-ROM of examples from O'Reilly books does require permission. Answering a question by citing this book and quoting example code does not require permission. Incorporating a significant amount of example code from this book into your product's documentation does require permission.

We appreciate, but do not require, attribution. An attribution usually includes the title, author, publisher, and ISBN. For example: *"Thoughtful Machine Learning* by Matthew Kirk (O'Reilly). Copyright 2015 Matthew Kirk, 978-1-449-37406-8."

If you feel your use of code examples falls outside fair use or the permission given above, feel free to contact us at *permissions@oreilly.com*.

Safari® Books Online

 *Safari Books Online* is an on-demand digital library that delivers expert content in both book and video form from the world's leading authors in technology and business.

Technology professionals, software developers, web designers, and business and creative professionals use Safari Books Online as their primary resource for research, problem solving, learning, and certification training.

Safari Books Online offers a range of plans and pricing for enterprise, government, education, and individuals.

Members have access to thousands of books, training videos, and prepublication manuscripts in one fully searchable database from publishers like O'Reilly Media, Prentice Hall Professional, Addison-Wesley Professional, Microsoft Press, Sams, Que, Peachpit Press, Focal Press, Cisco Press, John Wiley & Sons, Syngress, Morgan Kaufmann, IBM Redbooks, Packt, Adobe Press, FT Press, Apress, Manning, New Riders, McGraw-Hill, Jones & Bartlett, Course Technology, and hundreds more. For more information about Safari Books Online, please visit us online.

How to Contact Us

Please address comments and questions concerning this book to the publisher:

O'Reilly Media, Inc.
1005 Gravenstein Highway North
Sebastopol, CA 95472
800-998-9938 (in the United States or Canada)
707-829-0515 (international or local)
707-829-0104 (fax)

We have a web page for this book, where we list errata, examples, and any additional information. You can access this page at *http://bit.ly/thoughtful-machine-learning*.

To comment or ask technical questions about this book, send email to *bookques-tions@oreilly.com*.

For more information about our books, courses, conferences, and news, see our website at *http://www.oreilly.com*.

Find us on Facebook: *http://facebook.com/oreilly*

Follow us on Twitter: *http://twitter.com/oreillymedia*

Watch us on YouTube: *http://www.youtube.com/oreillymedia*

Acknowledgments

- Mike Loukides, who was intrigued by my idea about using test-driven development on machine learning code.
- Ann Spencer, my editor, who over the many months of my writing the book, coached me through edits and gave great feedback to shape the book.

I would like to thank all of the O'Reilly team, who helped make this book what it is, especially the following:

My reviewers:

- Brad Ediger, who was excited by my weird idea of writing a book on test-driven machine learning code, and gave great feedback on the first draft of the book.
- Starr Horne, who offered great insight during the review process. Thanks also for the conversation on the conference circuit about machine learning, error reporting, and more.
- Aaron Sumner, who provided great feedback about the overall coding structure of the book.

My amazing coworkers and friends who offered guidance during the book writing process: Edward Carrel, Jon-Michael Deldin, Christopher Hobbs, Chris Kuttruff, Stefan Novak, Mike Perham, Max Spransy, Moxley Stratton, and Wafa Zouyed.

This book would not be a reality without the consistent and pressing support of my family:

- To my wife, Sophia, who has been the anchor to my dreams and helped me shape the idea of this book into a reality.
- To my grandmother, Gail, who instilled a love of learning in me from an early age, and asked intently about the coffee book I was reading during a road trip (it was a book on Java).
- To my parents, Jay and Carol, who taught me the most about dissecting systems and adding human emotion to them.
- To my brother, Jacob, and nieces, Zoe and Darby, who are teaching me to relearn the world through a toddler's mind.

Lastly, I dedicate this book to science and the pursuit of knowledge.

## CHAPTER 1

Test-Driven Machine Learning

A great scientist is a dreamer and a skeptic. In modern history, scientists have made exceptional breakthroughs like discovering gravity, going to the moon, and producing the theory of relativity. All those scientists had something in common: they dreamt big. However, they didn't accomplish their feats without testing and validating their work first.

Although we aren't in the company of Einstein and Newton these days, we are in the age of big data. With the rise of the information age, it has become increasingly important to find ways to manipulate that data into something meaningful—which is precisely the goal of data science and machine learning.

Machine learning has been a subject of interest because of its ability to use information to solve complex problems like facial recognition or handwriting detection. Many times, machine learning algorithms do this by having tests baked in. Examples of these tests are formulating statistical hypotheses, establishing thresholds, and minimizing mean squared errors over time. Theoretically, machine learning algorithms have built a solid foundation. These algorithms have the ability to learn from past mistakes and minimize errors over time.

However, as humans, we don't have the same rate of effectiveness. The algorithms are capable of minimizing errors, but sometimes we may not point them toward minimizing the right errors, or we may make errors in our own code. Therefore, we need tests for addressing human error, as well as a way to document our progress. The most popular way of writing these tests is called *test-driven development* (TDD). This method of writing tests first has become popularized as a best practice for programmers. However, it is a best practice that is sometimes not exercised in a development environment.

There are two good reasons to use test-driven development. One reason is that while TDD takes 15–35% more time in active development mode, it also has the ability to reduce bugs up to 90% (*http://bit.ly/YLLBvs*). The second main reason to use TDD is for the benefit of documenting how the code is intended to work. As code becomes more complex, the need for a specification increases—especially as people are making bigger decisions based on what comes out of the analysis.

Harvard scholars Carmen Reinhart and Kenneth Rogoff wrote an economics paper stating that countries that took on debt of over 90% of their gross domestic product suffered sharp drops in economic growth. Paul Ryan cited this conclusion heavily in his presidential race. In 2013, three researchers from the University of Massachusetts found that the calculation was incorrect because it was missing a substantial number of countries from its analysis.

Some examples aren't as drastic, but this case demonstrates the potential blow to one's academic reputation due to a single error in the statistical analysis. One mistake can cascade into many more—and this is the work of Harvard researchers who have been through a rigorous process of peer review and have years of experience in research. It can happen to anybody. Using TDD would have helped to mitigate the risk of making such an error, and would have saved these researchers from the embarrassment.

History of Test-Driven Development

In 1999, Kent Beck popularized TDD through his work with extreme programming. TDD's power comes from the ability to first define our intentions and then satisfy those intentions. The practice of TDD involves writing a failing test, writing the code that makes it pass, and then refactoring the original code. Some people call it "red-green-refactor" after the colors of many testing libraries. Red is writing a test that doesn't work originally but documents what your goal is, while green involves making the code work so the test passes. Finally, you refactor the original code to work so that you are happy with its design.

Testing has always been a mainstay in the traditional development practice, but TDD emphasizes testing first instead of testing near the end of a development cycle. In a waterfall model, acceptance tests are used and involve many people—usually end users, not programmers—after the code is actually written. This approach seems good until coverage becomes a factor. Many times, quality assurance professionals test only what they want to test and don't get to everything underneath the surface.

TDD and the Scientific Method

Part of the reason why TDD is so appealing is that it syncs well with people and their working style. The process of hypothesizing, testing, and theorizing makes it very similar to the scientific method.

Science involves trial and error. Scientists come up with a hypothesis, test that hypothesis, and then combine their hypotheses into a theory.

 Hypothesize, test, and theorize could be called "red-green-refactor" instead.

Just as with the scientific method, writing tests first works well with machine learning code. Most machine learning practitioners apply some form of the scientific method, and TDD forces you to write cleaner and more stable code. Beyond its similarity to the scientific method, though, there are three other reasons why TDD is really just a *subset* of the scientific method: making a logical proposition of validity, sharing results through documentation, and working in feedback loops.

The beauty of test-driven development is that you can utilize it to experiment as well. Many times, we write tests first with the idea that we will eventually fix the error that is created by the initial test. But it doesn't have to be that way: you can use tests to experiment with things that might not ever work. Using tests in this way is very useful for many problems that aren't easily solvable.

TDD Makes a Logical Proposition of Validity

When scientists use the scientific method, they are trying to solve a problem and prove that it is valid. Solving a problem requires creative guessing, but without justification it is just a belief.

Knowledge, according to Plato, is a justified true belief and we need both a true belief and justification for that. To justify our beliefs, we need to construct a stable, logical proposition. In logic, there are two types of conditions to use for proposing whether something is true: necessary and sufficient conditions.

Necessary conditions are those without which our hypothesis fails. For example, this could be a unanimous vote or a preflight checklist. The emphasis here is that all conditions must be satisfied to convince us that whatever we are testing is correct.

Sufficient conditions, unlike necessary conditions, mean that there is enough evidence for an argument. For instance, thunder is sufficient evidence that lightning has happened because they go together, but thunder isn't necessary for lightning to happen. Many times sufficient conditions take the form of a statistical hypothesis. It might not be perfect, but it is sufficient enough to prove what we are testing.

Together, necessary and sufficient conditions are what scientists use to make an argument for the validity of their solutions. Both the scientific method and TDD use these religiously to make a set of arguments come together in a cohesive way. However, while the scientific method uses hypothesis testing and axioms, TDD uses integration and unit tests (see Table 1-1).

Table 1-1. A comparison of TDD to the scientific method

	Scientific method	TDD
Necessary conditions	Axioms	Pure functional testing
Sufficient conditions	Statistical hypothesis testing	Unit and integration testing

Example: Proof through axioms and functional tests

Fermat famously conjectured in 1637 that "there are no positive integers a, b, and c that can satisfy the equation $a^n + b^n = c^n$ for any integer value of n greater than two." On the surface, this appears like a simple problem, and supposedly Fermat himself said he had a proof. Except the proof was too big for the margin of the book he was working out of.

For 358 years, this problem was toiled over. In 1995, Andrew Wiles solved it using Galois transformations and elliptic curves. His 100-page proof was not elegant but was sound. Each section took a previous result and applied it to the next step.

The 100 pages of proof were based on axioms or presumptions that had been proved before, much like a functional testing suite would have been done. In programming terms, all of those axioms and assertions that Andrew Wiles put into his proof could have been written as functional tests. These functional tests are just coded axioms and assertions, each step feeding into the next section.

This vacuum of testing in most cases doesn't exist in production. Many times the tests we are writing are scattershot assertions about the code. In many cases, we are testing the thunder, not the lightning, to use our earlier example (i.e., our testing focuses on sufficient conditions, not necessary conditions).

Example: Proof through sufficient conditions, unit tests, and integration tests

Unlike pure mathematics, sufficient conditions are focused on just enough evidence to support a causality. An example is inflation. This mysterous force in economics has been studied since the 19th century. The problem with proving that inflation exists is that we cannot use axioms.

Instead, we rely on the sufficient evidence from our observations to prove that inflation exists. Based on our experience looking at economic data and separating out factors we know to be true, we have found that economies tend to grow over time. Sometimes they deflate as well. The existence of inflation can be proved purely on our previous observations, which are consistent.

Sufficient conditions like this have an analog to integration tests. Integration tests aim to test the overarching behavior of a piece of code. Instead of monitoring little changes, integration tests will watch the entire program and see whether the intended behavior is still there. Likewise, if the economy were a program we could assert that inflation or deflation exists.

TDD Involves Writing Your Assumptions Down on Paper or in Code

Academic institutions require professors to publish their research. While many complain that universities focus too much on publications, there's a reason why: publications are the way research becomes timeless. If professors decided to do their research in solitude and made exceptional breakthroughs but didn't publish, that research would be worthless.

Test-driven development is the same way: tests can be great in peer reviews as well as serving as a version of documentation. Many times, in fact, documentation isn't necessary when TDD is used. Software is abstract and always changing, so if someone doesn't document or test his code it will most likely be changed in the future. If there isn't a test ensuring that the code operates a certain way, then when a new programmer comes to work on the software she will probably change it.

TDD and Scientific Method Work in Feedback Loops

Both the scientific method and TDD work in feedback loops. When someone makes a hypothesis and tests it, he finds out more information about the problem he's investigating. The same is true with TDD; someone makes a test for what he wants and then as he goes through writing code he has more information as to how to proceed.

Overall, TDD is a type of scientific method. We make hypotheses, test them, and then revisit them. This is the same approach that TDD practitioners take with writing a test that fails first, finding the solution to it, and then refactoring that solution.

Example: Peer review

Peer review is common across many fields and formats, whether they be academic journals, books, or programming. The reason editors are so valuable is because they are a third party to a piece of writing and can give objective feedback. The counterpart in the scientific community is peer reviewing journal articles.

Test-driven development is different in that the third party is a program. When someone writes tests, the program codes the assumptions and requirements and is entirely objective. This feedback can be valuable for the programmer to test assumptions before someone else looks at the code. It also helps with reducing bugs and feature misses.

This doesn't mitigate the inherent issues with machine learning or math models; rather, it just defines the process of tackling problems and finding a good enough solution to them.

Risks with Machine Learning

While the scientific method and TDD are a good start to the development process, there are still issues that we might come across. Someone can follow the scientific method and still have wrong results; TDD just helps us create better code and be more objective. The following sections will outline some of these more commonly encountered issues with machine learning:

- Unstable data
- Underfitting
- Overfitting
- Unpredictable future

Unstable Data

Machine learning algorithms do their best to avoid unstable data by minimizing outliers, but what if the errors were our own fault? If we are misrepresenting what is correct data, then we will end up skewing our results.

This is a real problem considering the amount of incorrect information we may have. For example, if an application programming interface (API) you are using changes from giving you 0 to 1 binary information to –1 to 1, then that could be detrimental to the output of the model. We might also have holes in a time series of data. With this instability, we need a way of testing for data issues to mitigate human error.

Underfitting

Underfitting is when a model doesn't take into account enough information to accurately model real life. For example, if we observed only two points on an exponential curve, we would probably assert that there is a linear relationship there (Figure 1-1). But there may not be a pattern, because there are only two points to reference.

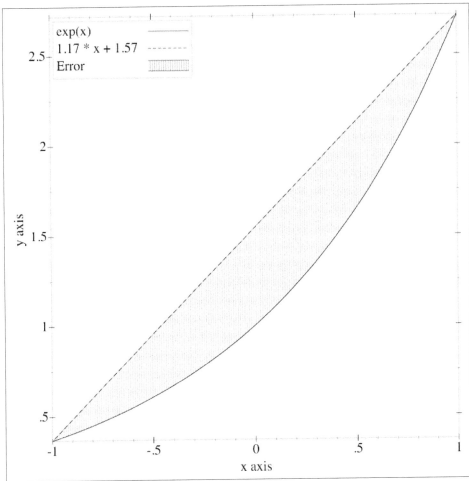

Figure 1-1. In the range of –1 to 1 a line will fit an exponential curve well

Unfortunately, though, when you increase the range you won't see nearly as clear results, and instead the error will drastically increase (Figure 1-2).

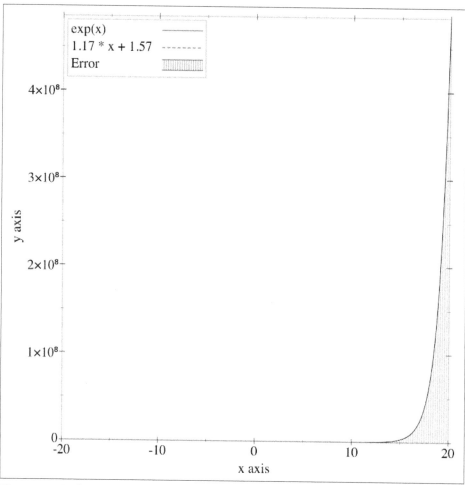

Figure 1-2. In the range of -20 to 20 a linear line will not fit an exponential curve at all

In statistics, there is a measure called *power* that denotes the probability of not finding a false negative. As power goes up, false negatives go down. However, what influences this measure is the sample size. If our sample size is too small, we just don't have enough information to come up with a good solution.

Overfitting

While too little of a sample isn't ideal, there is also some risk of overfitting data. Using the same exponential curve example, let's say we have 300,00 data points. Overfitting the model would be building a function that has 300,000 operators in it, effectively memorizing the data. This is possible, but it wouldn't perform very well if there were a new data point that was out of that sample.

It seems that the best way to mitigate underfitting a model is to give it more information, but this actually can be a problem as well. More data can mean more noise and more problems. Using too much data and too complex of a model will yield something that works for that particular data set and nothing else.

Unpredictable Future

Machine learning is well suited for the unpredictable future, because most algorithms learn from new information. But as new information is found, it can also come in unstable forms, and new issues can arise that weren't thought of before. We don't know what we don't know. When processing new information, it's sometimes hard to tell whether our model is working.

What to Test for to Reduce Risks

Given the fact that we have problems such as unstable data, underfitted models, overfitted models, and uncertain future resiliency, what should we do? There are some general guidelines and techniques, known as heuristics, that we can write into tests to mitigate the risk of these issues arising.

Mitigate Unstable Data with Seam Testing

In his book *Working Effectively with Legacy Code* (Prentice Hall), Michael Feathers introduces the concept of testing seams when interacting with legacy code. Seams are simply the points of integration between parts of a code base. In legacy code, many times we are given a piece of code where we don't know what it does internally but can predict what will happen when we feed it something. Machine learning algorithms aren't legacy code, but they are similar. As with legacy code, machine learning algorithms should be treated like a black box.

Data will flow into a machine learning algorithm and flow out of the algorithm. We can test those two seams by unit testing our data inputs and outputs to make sure they are valid within our given tolerances.

Example: Seam testing a neural network

Let's say that you would like to test a neural network. You know that the data that is yielded to a neural network needs to be between 0 and 1 and that in your case you want the data to sum to 1. When data sums to 1, that means it is modeling a percentage. For instance, if you have two widgets and three whirligigs, the array of data would be 2/5 widgets and 3/5 whirligigs. Because we want to make sure that we are feeding only information that is positive and adds up to 1, we'd write the following test in our test suite:

```
it 'needs to be between 0 and 1' do
  @weights = NeuralNetwork.weights
  @weights.each do |point|
    (0..1).must_include(point)
  end
end

it 'has data that sums up to 1' do
  @weights = NeuralNetwork.weights
  @weights.reduce(&:+).must_equal 1
end
```

Seam testing serves as a good way to define interfaces between pieces of code. While this is a trivial example, note that the more complex the data gets, the more important these seam tests are. As new programmers touch the code, they might not know all the intricacies that you do.

Check Fit by Cross-Validating

Cross-validation is a method of splitting all of your data into two parts: training and validation (see Figure 1-3). The training data is used to build the machine learning model, whereas the validation data is used to validate that the model is doing what is expected. This increases our ability to find and determine the underlying errors in a model.

Training is special to the machine learning world. Because machine learning algorithms aim to map previous observations to outcomes, training is essential. These algorithms learn from data that has been collected, so without an initial set to train on, the algorithm would be useless.

Swapping training with validation helps increase the number of tests. You would do this by splitting the data into two; the first time you'd use set 1 to train and set 2 to validate, and then you'd swap them for the second test. Depending on how much data you have, you could split the data into smaller sets and cross-validate that way. If you have enough data, you could split cross-validation into an indefinite amount of sets.

In most cases, people decide to split validation and training data in half—one part to train the model and the other to validate that it works with real data. If, for instance, you are training a language model that tags many parts of speech using a Hidden Markov Model, you want to minimize the error of the model.

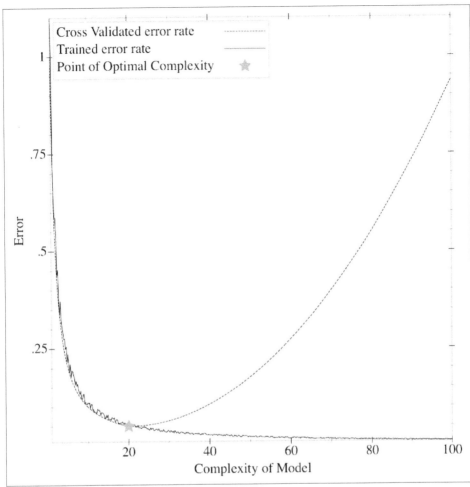

Figure 1-3. Our real goal is to minimize the cross-validated error or real error rate

Example: Cross-validating a model

From our trained model we might have a 5% error rate, but when we introduce data outside of the model, that error might skyrocket to something like 15%. That is why it's important to use a data set that is separate; this is as essential to machine learning as double-entry accounting is to accounting. For example:

```
def compare(network, text_file)
  misses = 0
  hits = 0

  sentences.each do |sentence|
    if model.run(sentence).classification == sentence.classification
      hits += 1
```

```
      else
        misses += 1
      end
    end

    assert misses < (0.05 * (misses + hits))
  end

  def test_first_half
    compare(first_data_set, second_data_set)
  end

  def test_second_half
    compare(second_data_set, first_data_set)
  end
```

This method of first splitting data into two sets eliminates common issues that might happen as a result of improper parameters on your machine learning model. It's a great way of finding issues before they become a part of any code base.

Reduce Overfitting Risk by Testing the Speed of Training

Occam's Razor emphasizes simplicity when modeling data, and states that the simpler solution is the better one. This directly implies "don't overfit your data." The idea that the simpler solution is the better one has to do with how overfitted models generally just memorize the data given to them. If a simpler solution can be found, it will notice the patterns versus parsing out the previous data.

A good proxy for complexity in a machine learning model is how fast it takes to train it. If you are testing different approaches to solving a problem and one takes 3 hours to train while the other takes 30 minutes, generally speaking the one that takes less time to train is probably better. The best approach would be to wrap a benchmark around the code to find out if it's getting faster or slower over time.

Many machine learning algorithms have max iterations built into them. In the case of neural networks, you might set a max epoch of 1,000 so that if the model isn't trained within 1,000 iterations, it isn't good enough. An epoch is just a measure of one iteration through all inputs going through the network.

Example: Benchmark testing

To take it a step further, you can also use unit testing frameworks like MiniTest. This adds computational complexity and an IPS (iterations per second) benchmark test to your test suite so that the performance doesn't degrade over time. For example:

```
it 'should not run too much slower than last time' do
  bm = Benchmark.measure do
    model.run('sentence')
  end
```

```
    bm.real.must_be < (time_to_run_last_time * 1.2)
  end
```

In this case, we don't want the test to run more than 20% over what it did last time.

Monitor for Future Shifts with Precision and Recall

Precision and recall are ways of monitoring the power of the machine learning implementation. Precision is a metric that monitors the percentage of true positives. For example, a precision of 4/7 would mean that 4 were correct out of 7 yielded to the user. Recall is the ratio of true positives to true positive plus false negatives. Let's say that we have 4 true positives and 9; in that case, recall would be 4/9.

User input is needed to calculate precision and recall. This closes the learning loop and improves data over time due to information feeding back after being misclassified. Netflix, for instance, illustrates this by displaying a star rating that it predicts you'd give a certain movie based on your watch history. If you don't agree with it and rate it differently or indicate you're not interested, Netflix feeds that back into its model for future predictions.

Conclusion

Machine learning is a science and requires an objective approach to problems. Just like the scientific method, test-driven development can aid in solving a problem. The reason that TDD and the scientific method are so similar is because of these three shared characteristics:

- Both propose that the solution is logical and valid.
- Both share results through documentation and work over time.
- Both work in feedback loops.

But while the scientific method and test-driven development are similar, there are some issues specific to machine learning:

- Unstable data
- Underfitting
- Overfitting
- Unpredictable future

Fortunately, these challenges can be mitigated through the heuristics shown in Table 1-2.

Table 1-2. Heuristics to mitigate machine learning risks

Problem/risk	Heuristic
Unstable data	Seam testing
Underfitting	Cross-validation
Overfitting	Benchmark testing (Occam's Razor)
Unpredictable future	Precision/recall tracking over time

The best part is that you can write and think about all of these heuristics before writing actual code. Test-driven development, like the scientific method, is valuable as a way to approach machine learning problems.

## CHAPTER 2

A Quick Introduction to Machine Learning

You've picked up this book because you're interested in machine learning. While you probably have an idea of what machine learning is, it's a subject that is often defined in a somewhat vague way. In this quick introduction, we'll go over what exactly machine learning is, as well as a general framework for thinking about machine learning algorithms.

What Is Machine Learning?

Machine learning is the intersection between theoretically sound computer science and practically noisy data. Essentially, it's about machines making sense out of data in much the same way that humans do.

Machine learning is a type of artificial intelligence whereby an algorithm or method will extract patterns out of data. Generally speaking, there are a few problems machine learning tackles; these are listed in Table 2-1 and described in the subsections that follow.

Table 2-1. The problems of machine learning

The problem	Machine learning category
Fitting some data to a function or function approximation	Supervised learning
Figuring out what the data is without any feedback	Unsupervised learning
Playing a game with rewards and payoffs	Reinforcement learning

Supervised Learning

Supervised learning, or function approximation, is simply fitting data to a function of any variety. For instance, given the noisy data shown in Figure 2-1, you can fit a line that generally approximates it.

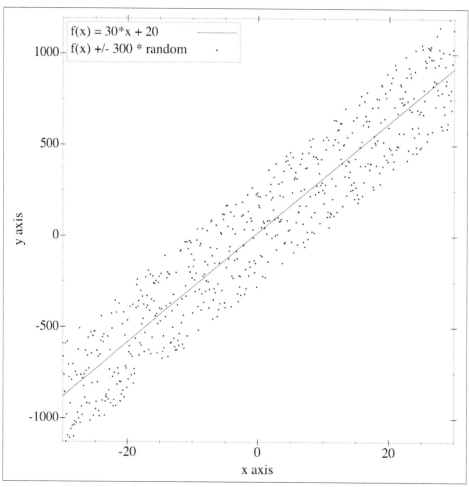

Figure 2-1. This shows a line fitted to some random data

Unsupervised Learning

Unsupervised learning involves figuring out what makes the data special. For instance, if we were given many data points, we could group them by similarity (Figure 2-2), or perhaps determine which variables are better than others.

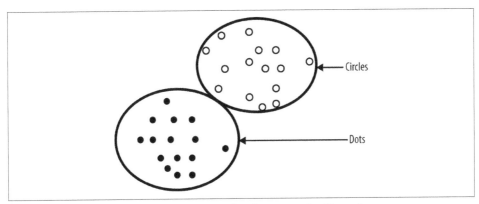

Figure 2-2. Clustering is a common example of unsupervised learning

Reinforcement Learning

Reinforcement learning involves figuring out how to play a multistage game with rewards and payoffs. Think of it as the algorithms that optimize the life of something. A common example of a reinforcement learning algorithm is a mouse trying to find cheese in a maze. For the most part, the mouse gets zero reward until it finally finds the cheese.

We will discuss supervised and unsupervised learning in this book but skip reinforcement learning. In the final chapter, I include some resources that you can check out if you'd like to learn more about reinforcement learning.

What Can Machine Learning Accomplish?

What makes machine learning unique is its ability to optimally figure things out. But each machine learning algorithm has quirks and trade-offs. Some do better than others. This book covers quite a few algorithms, so Table 2-2 provides a matrix to help you navigate them and determine how useful each will be to you.

Table 2-2. Machine learning algorithm matrix

Algorithm	Type	Class	Restriction bias	Preference bias
K-Nearest Neighbor	Supervised learning	Instance based	Generally speaking, KNN is good for measuring distance-based approximations, but it suffers from the curse of dimensionality	Prefers problems that are distance based
Naive Bayesian Classification	Supervised learning	Probabilistic	Works on problems where the inputs are independent from each other	Prefers problems where the probability will always be greater than zero for each class

Algorithm	Type	Class	Restriction bias	Preference bias
Hidden Markov Models	Supervised/ unsupervised	Markovian	Generally works well for system information where the Markov assumption holds	Prefers time series data and memory-less information
Support Vector Machine	Supervised learning	Decision boundary	Works where there is a definite distinction between two classifications	Prefers binary classification problems
Neural Networks	Supervised learning	Nonlinear functional approximation	Has little restriction bias	Prefers binary inputs
Clustering	Unsupervised	Clustering	No restriction	Prefers data that is in groupings given some form of distance (Euclidean, Manhattan, or others)
(Kernel) Ridge Regression	Supervised	Regression	Has low restriction on problems it can solve	Prefers continuous variables
Filtering	Unsupervised	Feature transformation	No restriction	Prefer data to have lots of variables on which to filter

Refer to this matrix throughout the book to understand how these algorithms relate to one another.

Machine learning is only as good as what it applies to, so let's get to implementing some of these algorithms!

 Before we get started, you will need to install Ruby, which you can do at *https://www.ruby-lang.org/en/*. This book was tested using Ruby 2.1.2, but things do change rapidly in the Ruby community. All of those changes will be annotated in the coding resources, which are available on GitHub (*https://github.com/thoughtfulml/ examples*).

Mathematical Notation Used Throughout the Book

This book uses mathematics to solve problems, but all of the examples are programmer-centric. Throughout the book, I'll use the mathematical notations shown in Table 2-3.

Table 2-3. Mathematical notations used in this book's examples

Symbol	How do you say it?	What does it do?
$\sum_{i=0}^{2} x_i$	The sum of all x's from x_0 to x_2	This is the same thing as $x_0 + x_1 + \ldots + x_2$.
$|x|$	The absolute value of x	This takes any value of x and makes it positive. So $x=-1$ would equal 1, and $x=1$ would equal 1 as well.
$\sqrt{4}$	The square root of 4	This is the opposite of 2^2.
$z_k = \;<0.5,\; 0.5>$	Vector z_k equals 0.5 and 0.5	This is a point on the xy plane and is denoted as a vector, which is a group of numerical points.
$log_2(2)$	Log 2	This solves for i in $2^i = 2$.
$P(A)$	Probability of A	In many cases, this is the count of A divided by the total occurrences.
$P(A|B)$	Probability of A given B	This is the probability of A and B divided by the probability of B.
$\{1,2,3\} \cap \{1\}$	The intersection of set one and two	This turns into a set called 1.
$\{1,2,3\} \cup \{4,1\}$	The union of set one and two	This equates to $\{1,2,3,4\}$.
$det(C)$	The determinant of the matrix C	This will help determine whether a matrix is invertible or not.
$a \propto b$	a is proportional to b	This means that $m\dot{a} = b$.
$min\ f(x)$	Minimize $f(x)$	This is an objective function to minimize the function $f(x)$.
X^T	Transpose of the matrix X	Take all elements of the matrix and switch the row with the column.

Conclusion

This isn't an exhaustive introduction to machine learning, but that's OK. There's always going to be a lot for us all to learn when it comes to this complex subject, but for the remainder of this book, this should serve us well in approaching these problems.

## CHAPTER 3

K-Nearest Neighbors Classification

You probably know someone who really likes a certain brand, such as a particular technology company or clothing manufacturer. Usually you can detect this by what the person wears, talks about, and interacts with. But what are some other ways we could determine brand affinity?

For an ecommerce site, we could identify brand loyalty by looking at previous orders of similar users to see what they've bought. So, for instance, let's assume that a user has a history of orders, each including two items, as shown in Figure 3-1.

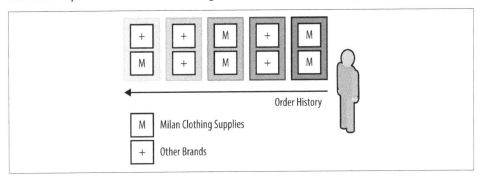

Figure 3-1. User with a history of orders of multiple brands

Based on his previous orders, we can see that this user buys a lot of Milan Clothing Supplies (not a real brand, but you get the picture). Out of the last five orders, he has bought five Milan Clothing Supplies shirts. Thus, we could say he has a certain affinity toward this company. Knowing this, if we pose the question of what brand this user is particularly interested in, Milan Clothing Supplies would be at the top.

This general idea is known as the *K-Nearest Neighbors* (KNN) classification algorithm. In our case, *K* equals 5, and each order represents a vote on a brand. Whatever brand gets the highest vote is our classification. This chapter will introduce and define the KNN classification as well as work through a code example that detects whether a face has glasses or facial hair.

 K-Nearest Neighbors classification is an instance-based supervised learning method that works well with distance-sensitive data. It suffers from the curse of dimensionality and other problems with distance-based algorithms as we'll discuss.

History of K-Nearest Neighbors Classification

The KNN algorithm was originally introduced by Drs. Evelyn Fix, and J.L. Hodges Jr, PhD, in an unpublished technical report (*http://1.usa.gov/1s3G4wX*) written for the U.S. Air Force School of Aviation Medicine. Fix and Hodges' original research focused on splitting up classification problems into a few subproblems:

- Distributions F and G are completely known.
- Distributions F and G are completely known except for a few parameters.
- F and G are unknown, except possibly for the existence of densities.

Fix and Hodges pointed out that if you know the distributions of two classifications or you know the distribution minus some parameters, you can easily back out useful solutions. Therefore, they focused their work on the more difficult case of finding classifications among distributions that are unknown. What they came up with laid the groundwork for the KNN algorithm.

This algorithm has been shown to have no worse than twice the Bayes error rate as data approaches infinity. This means that as entities are added to your data set, the rate of error will be no worse than a Bayes error rate. Also, being such a simple algorithm, KNN is easy to implement as a first stab at a classification problem, and is sufficient in many cases.

One challenge, though, is how arbitrary KNN can seem. How do you pick *K*? How do you determine what is a neighbor and what isn't? These are questions we'll aim to answer in the next couple of sections.

House Happiness Based on a Neighborhood

Imagine you are looking to buy a new house. You are considering two different houses and want to figure out whether the neighbors are happy or not. (Of course you don't want to move into an unhappy neighborhood.) You go around asking homeowners whether they are happy where they are and collect the information shown in Table 3-1.

We're going to use coordinate minutes because we want to make this specific to a small enough neighborhood.

Table 3-1. House happiness

Latitude minutes	Longitude minutes	Happy?
56	2	Yes
3	20	No
18	1	Yes
20	14	No
30	30	Yes
35	35	Yes

The two houses we are interested in are at (10,10) and (40,40). So which house is happy and which one is not? One method of determining this would be to use the nearest neighbor and determine whether they are happy. "Nearest" in this sense is absolute distance, which is also known as the Euclidean distance.

The Euclidean distance for a two-dimensional point like those shown in Table 3-1 would be $\sqrt{(x_1 - x_2)^2 + (y_1 - y_2)^2}$.

In Ruby, this would look like the following:

```ruby
require 'matrix'

# Euclidean distance between two vectors v1 and v2
# Note that Vector#magnitude is the same thing as the Euclidean distance
# from (0,0,....) to the vector point.
distance = ->(v1, v2) {
  (v1 - v2).magnitude
}

house_happiness = {
  Vector[56, 2] => 'Happy',
  Vector[3, 20] => 'Not Happy',
  Vector[18, 1] => 'Happy',
  Vector[20, 14] => 'Not Happy',
  Vector[30, 30] => 'Happy',
  Vector[35, 35] => 'Happy'
}
```

```
house_1 = Vector[10, 10]
house_2 = Vector[40, 40]

find_nearest = ->(house) {
  house_happiness.sort_by {|point,v|
    distance.(point, house)
  }.first
}

find_nearest.(house_1) #=> [Vector[20, 14], "Not Happy"]
find_nearest.(house_2) #=> [Vector[35, 35], "Happy"]
```

Based on this reasoning, you can see that the nearest neighbor for the first house is not happy, whereas the second house's neighbor is. But what if we increased the number of neighbors we looked at?

```
# Using same code from above in this as well

find_nearest_with_k = ->(house, k) {
  house_happiness.sort_by {|point, v|
    distance.(point, house)
  }.first(k)
}

find_nearest_with_k.(house_1, 3)
#=> [[Vector[20, 14], "Not Happy"], [Vector[18, 1], "Happy"], [Vector[3, 20], "N
ot Happy"]]
find_nearest_with_k.(house_2, 3)
#=> [[Vector[35, 35], "Happy"], [Vector[30, 30], "Happy"], [Vector[20, 14], "No
t Happy"]]
```

Using more neighbors doesn't change the classification! This is a good thing and increases our confidence in the classification. This method demonstrates the *K-Nearest Neighbors* classification. More or less, we take the *nearest* neighbors and use their attributes to come up with a score. In this case, we wanted to see whether one house would be happier than the other, but the data can really be anything.

KNN is an excellent algorithm because it is so simple, as you've just seen. It is also extremely powerful. It can be used to classify or regress data (see the following sidebar).

Classification and Regression

Note that in the preceding scenario we are mainly looking for whether the house is happy; that is, instead of trying to value the happiness, we are simply checking whether it meets our criteria. This is called a *classification problem*, and it can take many forms.

Many times classification problems are *binary*, meaning that they have only two possible answers, such as good or bad, true or false, and right or wrong. A lot of problems can be distilled into the binary category.

On the other hand, we could look for a numerical value of happiness for the house, but that would be *a regression problem*. While we won't cover regression problems in this chapter, we will return to them later when we talk about Kernel Ridge Regressions (i.e., fitting a function to calculate a continuous answer).

This chapter will cover quite a bit and is broken out into a few different concerns around using KNN. We will first discuss picking K, or the constant that determines your neighborhood. Then we'll delve more into what "nearest" means and follow up with an example of facial classification using OpenCV.

How Do You Pick K?

In the case of figuring out house happiness, we implicitly picked a K of 5. This works well when we are making a quick judgment based on a person's most recent purchases. But for bigger problems, we might not have the ability to guess.

K in the K-Nearest Neighbors algorithm is an arbitrary number generally ranging from 1 to the number of data points. With that much of a range, you might think that it's difficult to pick out the optimal K, but in practice it's not really such a vast decision. You have three primary options for choosing K:

- Guessing
- Using a heuristic
- Optimizing using an algorithm

Guessing K

Guessing is the easiest solution. In the case of classifying brands into groups, we just pick 11 as a good guess. We know that 11 orders is probably sufficient to get a good idea of how a person shops.

Many times when we are approaching a problem we can qualitatively come up with a good enough K to solve the problem, so guessing will work. If you want to be more scientific about it, however, there are a few heuristics that can help.

Heuristics for Picking K

There are three heuristics that can help you determine an optimal K for a KNN algorithm:

- Avoid an even K when there are only two classes to classify.
- Choose a K that is greater or equal to the number of classes plus one.
- Choose a K that is low enough to avoid noise.

Use coprime class and K combinations

Picking coprime numbers of classes and K will ensure fewer ties. Coprime numbers are simply two numbers that don't share any common divisors except for 1. So, for instance, 4 and 9 are coprime while 3 and 9 are not.

Imagine you have two classes, good and bad. If we were to pick a K of 6, which is even, then we might end up having ties. Graphically it looks like Figure 3-2.

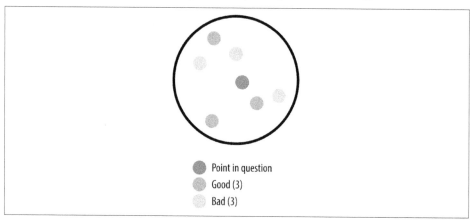

Figure 3-2. Tie with K=6 and two classes

If you picked a K of 5 instead (Figure 3-3), there wouldn't be a tie.

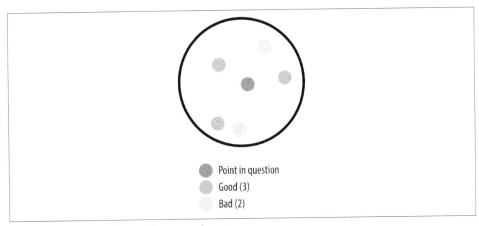

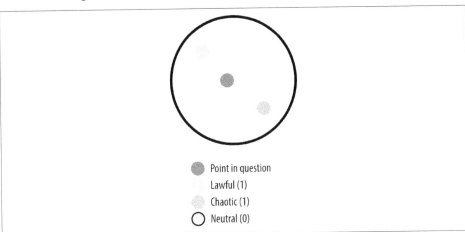

Figure 3-3. K=5 with two classes and no tie

Choose a K that is greater or equal to the number of classes + 1

Imagine there are three classes: lawful, chaotic, and neutral. A good heuristic is to pick a *K* of at least 3 because anything less will mean that there is no chance that each class will be represented.

To illustrate, Figure 3-4 shows the case of *K=2*.

Figure 3-4. With K=2 there is no possibility that all three classes will be represented

Note how there are only two classes that get the chance to be used. Again, this is why we need to use at least *K=3*. But based on what we found in the first heuristic, ties are not a good thing. So, really, instead of *K=3*, we should use *K=4* (as shown in Figure 3-5).

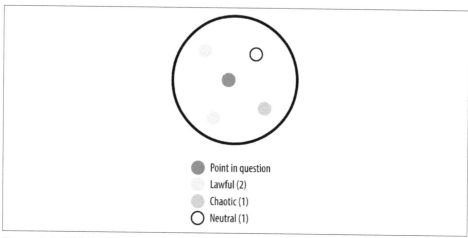

Figure 3-5. With K set greater than the number of classes, there is a chance for all classes to be represented

Choose a K that is low enough to avoid noise

As K increases, you eventually approach the size of the entire data set. If you were to pick the entire data set, you would select the most common class. To return to our brand affinity example, say you have 100 orders, as shown in Table 3-2.

Table 3-2. Brands ordered

Brand	Count
Widget Inc.	30
Bozo Group	23
Robots and Rockets	12
Ion 5	35
Total	100

If we were to set $K=100$, our answer will always be Ion 5 because Ion 5 is the distribution (the most common class) of the order history. That is not really what we want; instead, we want to determine the most recent order affinity. More specifically, we want to minimize the amount of noise that comes into our classification. Without coming up with a specific algorithm for this, we can justify K being set to a much lower rate, like $K=3$ or $K=11$.

Algorithms for Picking K

Picking K can be somewhat qualitative and nonscientific, and that's why there are many algorithms showing how to optimize K over a given training set. There are many approaches to choosing K, ranging from genetic algorithms to brute force to grid searches.

Many people assert that you should determine K based on *domain knowledge* that you have as the implementor. For instance, if you know that 5 is good enough, you can pick that.

This problem where you are trying to minimize error based on an arbitrary K is known as a *hill climbing problem*. The idea is to iterate through a couple of possible Ks until you find a suitable error. The difficult part about finding a K using an algorithm like genetic algorithms or brute force is that as K increases, the complexity of the classification also increases and slows down performance. In other words, as you increase K, the program actually gets slower.

> If you want to learn more about genetic algorithms applied to finding an optimal K, you can read more about it in Florian Nigsch et al.'s *Journal of Chemical Information and Modeling* article, "Melting Point Prediction Employing k-Nearest Neighbor Algorithms and Genetic Parameter Optimization" (*http://bit.ly/1q84Zb7*).

Personally, I think iterating twice through 1% of the population size is good enough. You should have a decent idea of what works and what doesn't just by experimenting with different Ks.

What Makes a Neighbor "Near"?

Imagine that you are sitting on the corner of a city block. How far is it from one corner of the block to the opposite corner?

The answer depends on your constraints: are you able to jump over fences on foot, or do you have to drive? If you were to drive you'd be traveling two times the length of the city block (Figure 3-6) whereas if you walked straight it'd be $\sqrt{2x^2}$ where x is the length of a city block (Figure 3-7). Assuming that a city block is 250 feet (76.2 meters) long, we could say that by car the distance would be 500 feet (152.4 meters), whereas on foot, it'd be roughly 353.5 feet (107.75 meters).

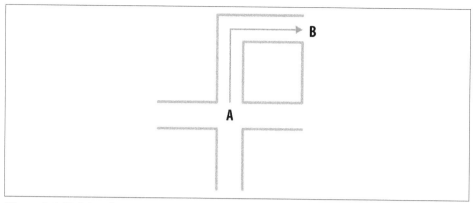

Figure 3-6. Driving from point A to point B on a city block

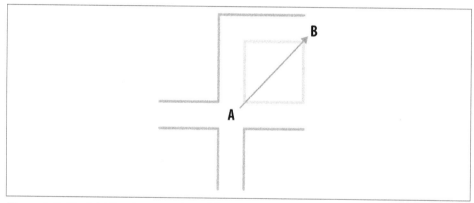

Figure 3-7. Straight line between A and B

You probably remember what we've just defined from geometry class. The Pythagorean theorem states that the length of a hypotenuse is $\sqrt{a^2 + b^2}$.

In modern mathematics terms, these are called *metrics*. They are a measure of how far points are from each other. We calculate these metrics using a distance function, which in the preceding example was the *Taxicab distance function* and *Euclidean distance function*. There are many ways of measuring distance, and how you do so is essential to understanding how the KNN algorithm works because it is based on proximity of data. For the most part, Euclidean distances are commonly used and represent the shortest path between two points.

Minkowski Distance

A generalization of Euclidean and Taxicab distances is called the *Minkowski distance*. To understand the Minkowski distance, let's first look at what the Taxicab distance function looks like:

$$d_{taxicab}(x, y) = \Sigma_{i=1}^{n} |x_i - y_i|$$

This function takes the absolute differences between all dimensions of the points x and y. Now let's look at the Euclidean distance function:

$$d_{euclid}(x, y) = \sqrt{\Sigma_{i=1}^{n} (x_i - y_i)^2}$$

Note that squaring something will always yield a positive number and that $\sqrt{x} = x^{\frac{1}{2}}$. So we could rewrite this to be:

$$d_{euclid}(x, y) = \left(\Sigma_{i=1}^{n} |x_i - y_i|^2\right)^{\frac{1}{2}}$$

This is very similar to the preceding Taxicab distance function, and in fact Minkowski generalizes this to the following:

$$d(x, y) = \left(\Sigma_{i=1}^{n} |x_i - y_i|^p\right)^{\frac{1}{p}}$$

Introducing a new parameter p, we can build the Taxicab distance function using $p=1$ and the Euclidean distance function using $p=2$. This is intriguing because if we needed we could increase p as much as we need to. While we won't get into the application of all versions of a Minkowski distance, you now have a foundation that you can opt to study more.

Mahalanobis Distance

One problem with the Minkowski type distance functions is that they assume that data should be symmetric in nature—that is, that distance is the same on all sides.

A lot of times, data is not spherical in nature or well suited for symmetric distances like the Minkowski distances. For example, in the case of Figure 3-8, we should take into consideration the ellipsoidal nature of the data. Instead of drawing a perfect circle around the data like the one shown, we need to figure something out that is better suited for the data's variability.

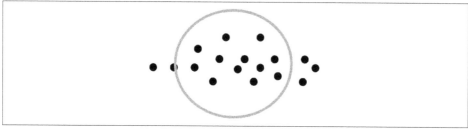

Figure 3-8. With squashed data, Minkowski distances don't work as well

The *Mahalanobis distance function* takes into consideration a volatility about each dimension (see Figure 3-9). So for each dimension of the data there is a certain variable s_i, which is the standard deviation of that set.

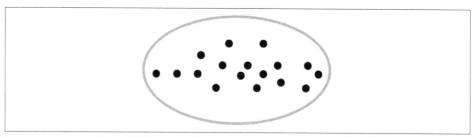

Figure 3-9. Using the Mahalanobis distance

The formula for the Mahalanobis distance is as follows:

$$d(x, y) = \sqrt{\Sigma_{i=1}^{n} \frac{(x_i - y_i)^2}{s_i^2}}$$

As you can see, this is very similar to the Euclidean distance, except it takes into consideration the given standard deviation of the dimensions.

Determining Classes

Classes can be quite arbitrary. Sometimes things aren't as mutually exclusive as we first think. So a caveat with building KNN classification tools is that as the number of attributes that you are modeling increases, the number of classes also increases exponentially.

For example, if we have two attribute colors, *red* and *yellow*, we end up with the classes red, yellow, and orange (see Figure 3-10).

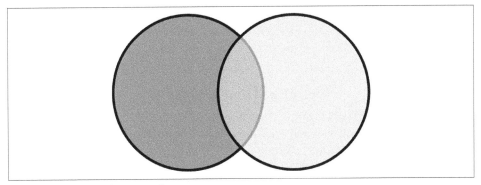

Figure 3-10. Mix of two attributes

Now if we add the attribute blue, we'll have red, yellow, blue, green, burnt sienna, orange, and purple classes (see Figure 3-11). In the first case, our two attributes yielded three classes, while in the second case our three attributes yielded seven classes.

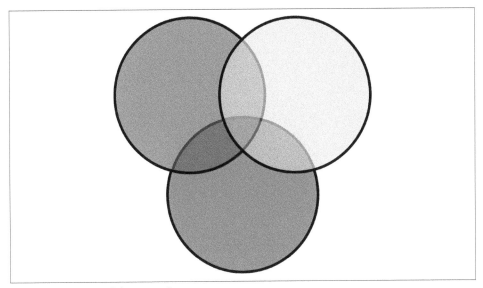

Figure 3-11. Mix of three attributes

The general case of combining attributes into mutually exclusive classes is n attributes the amount of class names will be: $2^n - 1$ where n is the amount of attributes you are adding.

Unless there's a strong argument for taking out mixed classes, this is an important distinction to make. If you have 4 attributes you can assume that there are 15 classes you need to take into consideration, so set your *K* to at least 16.

The Curse of Dimensionality

The *K*-Nearest Neighbors algorithm has one downside, which is called the *curse of dimensionality*. This curse is that high dimensional data tends to be sparse and far apart. Imagine a shotgun blast where over time the pellets expand through the air. This problem is common in algorithms that are based on locality and the ability to determine how close something is.

Figure 3-12 shows how a unit sphere (i.e., the distance from 0,0,0 to the edge is exactly 1), when shrunken onto a two-dimensional plane, actually gets a slightly less-than-average distance to points. The opposite happens when it's expanding into more dimensions.

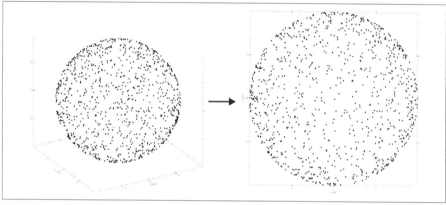

Figure 3-12. Curse of dimensionality on a sphere

There is no way of avoiding this with regards to the KNN algorithm itself; it has to be mitigated through other means, which we'll be covering in Chapter 6.

We will also discuss the curse of dimensionality in Chapters 9 and 10.

Beard and Glasses Detection Using KNN and OpenCV

Suppose that we wanted to determine with a general accuracy whether someone had facial hair and whether he was wearing glasses. How would we do such a thing? We really don't have a lot of information about the distribution of any of this data, so KNN is a good algorithm to use, along with some help from OpenCV (Open Computer Vision). First I'll explain what the program's class diagram looks like. From

---

there, we'll delve deeper into how to convert a raw image into an avatar. Then we'll extract features from those avatar images. When we have enough features, we'll then use KNN to build a neighborhood of faces that will help us determine attributes of input images.

Setup notes

All of the code for this example can be found on GitHub (*http://bit.ly/1m8MMiL*).

Because Ruby is constantly changing, the *README* file should include the most up-to-date instructions on getting these code examples working.

You will have to install imagemagick, OpenCV, and a recent Ruby version to get started.

The Class Diagram

The general idea for this example is to take a raw image (`Image`), extract a smaller avatar image (`Face`), and then put all the `Face` classes inside of a `Neighborhood` comprising faces that have been annotated with information. See Figure 3-13 for the class diagram.

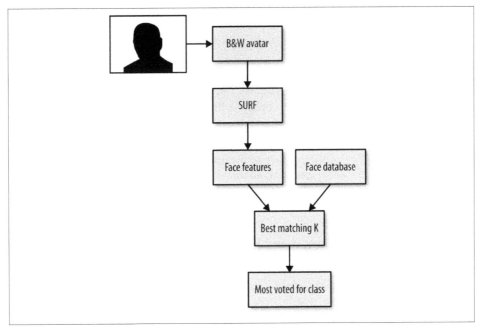

Figure 3-13. Class diagram for our facial hair and glasses detector

Raw Image to Avatar

The `Image` class takes a raw image of a human and tries to find a face inside it. To accomplish this, we rely on OpenCV. What we want is something like the images shown in Figures 3-14 and 3-15.

Figure 3-14. Raw image that gets extracted

Figure 3-15. Extracted avatar from Haar classifier

Knowing a bit about OpenCV, we realize that we can achieve this by using a Haar-like feature to extract what looks like a face. We use data provided by the OpenCV library and rely on its implementation to accomplish this.

 This data is freely available and not actually made by me. Instead, someone trained this data set with facial images to figure out what looks like a face and what doesn't. It extracts some features on that face that were built by others.

OpenCV and Haar-Like Features

OpenCV is a tool that can extract faces out of a bigger image using a Haar-like feature, which is just a rectangle around something we want to isolate. Based on previous information, we know that faces, unlike background elements, generally share certain characteristics, so we can use Haar-like training information to determine the rectangle where the face exists.

For more information on OpenCV, check out these resources:

- *Mastering OpenCV Practical Computer Projects* (*http://amzn.to/1tHE4cd*) by Daniel Lélis Baggio (Packt Publishing)
- The OpenCV documentation (*http://docs.opencv.org*) is great as well.

To determine whether our avatars are correct, we use pHash. Unlike MD5 or SHA1, which are cryptographic hashes, this *perceptual* hash uses *hamming distances* to find close matches. So even though the photo is slightly off, it'll still be a duplicate.

 A hamming distance is the sum of differences in a string. For instance, if you have the strings `apple` and `oople`, the first two characters are different, so the hamming distance is 2. These distances work only on equal size strings.

To begin, we need to test whether our face extraction method will return the same photo every time. We do that by asserting that the top photo extracts the second:

```ruby
# test/lib/image_spec.rb
require 'spec_helper'

describe Image do
  it 'tries to convert to a face avatar using haar classifier' do
    @image = Image.new('./test/fixtures/raw.jpg')
    @face = @image.to_face

    avatar1 = Phashion::Image.new("./test/fixtures/avatar.jpg")
    avatar2 = Phashion::Image.new(@face.filepath)

    assert avatar1.duplicate?(avatar2)
  end
end
```

This will fail, as you can imagine, because `@image.to_face` does nothing and `@face` doesn't have a filepath associated with it.

To fill in the gaps, let's try the following:

```ruby
# lib/image.rb
# Stub out Face for now
Face = Struct.new(:filepath)

class Image
  HAAR_FILEPATH = './data/haarcascade_frontalface_alt.xml'
  FACE_DETECTOR = OpenCV::CvHaarClassifierCascade::load(HAAR_FILEPATH)

  attr_reader :filepath

  def initialize(filepath)
```

```ruby
    @filepath = filepath
  end

  def self.write(filepath)
    yield
    filepath
  end

  def face_region
    @image = OpenCV::CvMat.load(@filepath, OpenCV::CV_LOAD_IMAGE_GRAYSCALE)
    FACE_DETECTOR.detect_objects(@image).first
  end

  def to_face
    name = File.basename(@filepath)
    outfile = File.expand_path("../../public/faces/avatar_#{name}", __FILE__)

    self.class.write(outfile) do
      image = MiniMagick::Image.open(@filepath)
      image.crop(crop_params)
      image.write(outfile)
    end

    Face.new(outfile)
  end

  def x_size
    face_region.bottom_right.x - face_region.top_left.x
  end

  def y_size
    face_region.bottom_right.y - face_region.top_left.y
  end

  def crop_params
    crop_params = <<-EOL
      #{x_size - 1}x#{y_size-1}+#{face_region.top_left.x + 1}+#{face_region.top_
left.y + 1}
    EOL
  end
end
```

At this point, you can see we're using two libraries, MiniMagick and OpenCV, as well as *haarcascade_frontalface_alt.xml*, a training set from the OpenCV library that detects faces. Our tests should pass and we can assume that Image works as expected. But we need to now focus on making a Face class.

Features versus Dimensions versus Instances

Machine learning uses the terms *features*, *dimensions*, and *instances* often.

Features are a property of a given data set. Generally, they are important combinations of *dimensions*, which are the different sections of the data. Lastly, we have *instances*, which are a specific piece of data.

A good way of thinking about features versus dimensions would be lighting in a room (Table 3-3). Let's say you have three lights. There are eight possible combinations for the lighting in the room. But you really just want to know if the room is bright enough or not (which means there are at least two lights on).

Table 3-3. Lighting for the room

Light 1 on?	Light 2 on?	Light 3 on?	Light enough?
No	No	No	No
Yes	No	No	No
No	Yes	No	No
No	No	Yes	No
Yes	Yes	No	Yes
No	Yes	Yes	Yes
Yes	No	Yes	Yes
Yes	Yes	Yes	Yes

In this case, we have one *feature*—whether the room is light enough, which is based on the three *dimensions* of the lights being on or off. The *instances* are just the combinations of lights.

The Face Class

The Face class has one responsibility: to load an avatar image and extract features from it. These features will then interface with the Neighborhood class, which we will discuss in the next section. This is where things become more difficult because features can be extracted in three different ways:

- Extracting the shades of each pixel (this is a grayscale image, so we use shades rather than colors)
- Using SIFT
- Using SURF

Extracting the shades of the image into a pixel-by-pixel matrix would be the naive approach and most likely would have us run into the curse of dimensionality. The naïveté would come from not reducing the amount of noisy pixels that mean nothing to us. Some algorithms would be able to handle grayscale inputs, like a Neural Network (which we will get to in Chapter 7). Deep learning, for instance, leverages this benefit of neural networks and is able to find features out of grayscale pixels.

Another method is using an algorithm called SIFT (Scale Invariant Feature Transform). This algorithm, which was built by David Lowe in 1999, is a computer vision algorithm for detecting important features. This algorithm also happens to be patented by the University of British Columbia. This is a big improvement over pixel-by-pixel matrices.

There is a similar algorithm called SURF (Speeded Up Robust Features). SURF was proposed by Herbert Bay in 2006 and is an improvement over SIFT because it is quite fast. This algorithm has proven quite successful at recognizing many features of images.

SIFT or SURF would both be good choices to go with. OpenCV has a good implementation of SURF, so that is what we will use to extract our features from avatars.

Testing the Face class

SURF gives us two pieces of information about the Face class: key points and descriptors. Key points are points in two-dimensional space (x,y pairs). Descriptors are more interesting because they contain either a 64- or 128-pixel-wide vector of characteristics about the feature. Instead of testing how well the SURF algorithm detects features, we need to ensure that the data is always the same, meaning that two Face classes should have the same features extracted.

A test for this would look like the following:

```
# test/lib/face_spec.rb
require 'spec_helper'
require 'matrix'

describe Face do
  let(:avatar_path) { './test/fixtures/avatar.jpg' }

  it 'has the same descriptors for the exact same face' do
    @face_descriptors = Face.new(avatar_path).descriptors
    @face2_descriptors = Face.new(avatar_path).descriptors
```

```
    @face_descriptors.sort_by! { |row| Vector[*row].magnitude }
    @face2_descriptors.sort_by! { |row| Vector[*row].magnitude }

    @face_descriptors.zip(@face2_descriptors).each do |f1, f2|
      assert (0.99..1.01).include?(cosine_similarity(f1, f2)),
        "Face descriptors don't match"
    end
  end

  it 'has the same keypoints for the exact same face' do
    @face = Face.new(avatar_path)
    @face2 = Face.new(avatar_path)

    # This is purely because Ruby's implementation of OpenCV doesn't
    # Have a representation of == for SurfPoints :(
    @face.keypoints.each_with_index do |kp, i|
      f1 = Vector[kp.pt.x, kp.pt.y]
      f2 = Vector[@face2.keypoints[i].pt.x, @face2.keypoints[i].pt.y]

      assert (0.99..1.01).include?(cosine_similarity(f1,f2)),
        "Face keypoints do not match"
    end
  end
end
```

Cosine Similarity

You'll notice that we're using a function called `cosine_similarity` here. This is a good way of determining how close something is. Instead of relying on the data being 100% equal, we can compare two vectors that are close enough.

Inside the *spec_helper.rb* file to implement this method, we would write:

```
# test/spec_helper.rb
def cosine_similarity(array_1, array_2)
  v1 = Vector[*array_1]
  v2 = Vector[*array_2]
  v1.inner_product(v2) / (v1.magnitude * v2.magnitude)
end
```

Cosine similarity is a useful measure of comparing two different vectors that need to be similar. It effectively measures the angle between the two vectors and not the magnitude. So, for instance, in this case, if we had [2,2] versus [1,1], we would see a cosine similarity of 1:

```
cosine_similarity([2,2], [1,1]) #=> 0.9999 ~ 1
```

Using cosine similarity is very useful for comparing two descriptors, such as faces, to see whether they are at least in the same direction.

Remember that our `Face` class before was a `Struct`, so we need to actually fill in those pieces:

```ruby
# lib/face.rb

class Face
  include OpenCV
  MIN_HESSIAN = 600

  attr_reader :filepath

  def initialize(filepath)
    @filepath = filepath
  end

  def descriptors
    @descriptors ||= features.last
  end

  def keypoints
    @keypoints ||= features.first
  end

  private
  def features
    image = CvMat.load(@filepath, CV_LOAD_IMAGE_GRAYSCALE)
    param = CvSURFParams.new(MIN_HESSIAN)
    @keypoints, @descriptors = image.extract_surf(param)
  end
end
```

As you can see, there's not a lot going on here except extracting key points and descriptors. MIN_HESSIAN is an arbitrary number that is recommended to be between 400 and 800. As the MIN_HESSIAN value increases, the number of features SURF will detect decreases, but those features will be more important. We are also extracting 64 dimensions out of each face.

We have taken our raw images and converted them into smaller avatars. And now we have a way of extracting a feature set out of them. So what's next?

The Neighborhood Class

At this point, we have enough information to build a `Neighborhood` class, which will find us the closest features, and tally attributes associated with the pictures in which those features are contained.

As you can see, we want to match each feature of the image to a big set of features. As soon as we find the closest K of those features, each one of those close features will have an image associated with it. And for all of those faces, there are associated attributes that we'll use to calculate the eventual classification.

Based on our previous knowledge of finding things that are close, we could approach this in many different ways. We could use a Mahalanobis distance, a Euclidean distance, or even a taxicab distance. We don't really know enough about the data, so we will go with the simplest, most common distance metric: Euclidean. This is a good generic distance function to use and could probably be revisited at a different time.

A K-D tree, or *K*-dimensional tree, is a data structure used to match vectors to a tree of vectors. You can utilize one to do a very quick nearest neighbor search using *K*-dimensions.

So we would first define our test to be:

```ruby
# test/lib/neighborhood_spec.rb

describe Neighborhood do
  it 'finds the nearest id for a given face' do
    files = ['./test/fixtures/avatar.jpg']
    n = Neighborhood.new(files)

    n.nearest_feature_ids(files.first, 1).each do |id|
      n.file_from_id(id).must_equal files.first
    end
  end
end
```

Filling in the blanks, we have a neighborhood that now looks like the following:

```ruby
# lib/neighborhood.rb

class Neighborhood
  def initialize(files)
    @ids = {}
    @files = files
    setup!
  end

  def file_from_id(id)
    @ids.fetch(id)
  end

  def nearest_feature_ids(file, k)
    desc = Face.new(file).descriptors

    ids = []

    desc.each do |d|
      ids.concat(@kd_tree.find_nearest(d, k).map(&:last))
    end
```

```
      ids.uniq
    end
  end
```

You'll notice that the ids are unique. That is because we need a unique set of features to match against and don't care about replacement in our feature set. Now that we have a neighborhood that works with a simple file, we need to annotate and actually use some real data; for that, we'll need a face database.

Bootstrapping the neighborhood with faces

To achieve what we want with our facial hair and glasses detection program, we need a set of faces with facial hair, with glasses, with both, and without either. For that, we have access to the AT&T facial database (*http://www.cl.cam.ac.uk/research/dtg/attarch ive/facedatabase.html*). This data contains 40 different people photographed 10 times each. There is no annotation on any of the pictures, so we can manually build JSON files called *attributes.json*. These sit at the root of each individual's folder of photos and takes the form of:

```
{
  "facial_hair": false,
  "glasses": false,
}
```

If there is a picture of a person with glasses and another picture of that person without glasses, we use the following type of *attributes.json*:

```
[{
  "ids": [1,2,5,6,7,8,9,10],
  "facial_hair": true,
  "glasses": true,
},
{
  "ids": [3,4],
  "facial_hair": true,
  "glasses": false,
}]
```

Note that we have an array with ids that split up the attributes. We need to write a test for attaching attributes to images:

```
# test/lib/neighborhood_spec.rb

describe Neighborhood do
  it 'returns attributes from given files' do
    files = ['./test/fixtures/avatar.jpg']

    n = Neighborhood.new(files)

    expected = {
      'fixtures' => JSON.parse(File.read('./test/fixtures/attributes.json'))
```

```
      }

      n.attributes.must_equal expected
    end
  end
```

For each folder, the attributes should be parsed and brought into a hash like so:

```
# lib/neighborhood.rb

class Neighborhood
  # initialize
  # file_from_id
  # nearest_feature_ids

  def attributes
    attributes = {}
    @files.each do |file|
      att_name = File.join(File.dirname(file), 'attributes.json')

      attributes[att_name.split("/")[-2]] = JSON.parse(File.read(att_name))
    end
    attributes
  end
end
```

But we're still missing one piece—a hash containing the tally of the different classes ("Facial Hair No Glasses," "Facial Hair Glasses," "Glasses No Facial Hair," "Glasses Facial Hair"). In our case, we'd like something like this:

```
{
  'glasses' => {false => 1, true => 0},
  'facial_hair' => {false => 1, true => 1}
}
```

That way, we can see the votes (counts) for each class broken out. A test for this would look as follows:

```
# test/lib/neighborhood.rb

describe Neighborhood do
  it 'finds the nearest face which is itself' do
    files = ['./test/fixtures/avatar.jpg']
    neighborhood = Neighborhood.new(files)

    descriptor_count = Face.new(files.first).descriptors.length
    attributes = JSON.parse(File.read('./test/fixtures/attributes.json'))

    expectation = {
      'glasses' => {
        attributes.fetch('glasses') => descriptor_count,
        !attributes.fetch('glasses') => 0
      },
```

```
      'facial_hair' => {
        attributes.fetch('facial_hair') => descriptor_count,
        !attributes.fetch('facial_hair') => 0
      }
    }

    neighborhood.attributes_guess(files.first).must_equal expectation
  end

  it 'returns the proper face class' do
    file = './public/att_faces/s1/1.png'
    attrs = JSON.parse(File.read('./public/att_faces/s1/attributes.json'))

    expectation = {'glasses' => false, 'facial_hair' => false}

    attributes = %w[glasses facial_hair]
    Neighborhood.face_class(file, attributes).must_equal expectation
  end
end
```

And filling in the pieces, we'd have this in our Neighborhood class:

```
# lib/neighborhood.rb

class Neighborhood
  # initialize
  # file_from_id
  # nearest_feature_ids
  # attributes

  def self.face_class(filename, subkeys)
    dir = File.dirname(filename)
    base = File.basename(filename, '.png')

    attributes_path = File.expand_path('../attributes.json', filename)
    json = JSON.parse(File.read(attributes_path))

    h = nil

    if json.is_a?(Array)
      h = json.find do |hh|
        hh.fetch('ids').include?(base.to_i)
      end or
      raise "Cannot find #{base.to_i} inside of #{json} for file #{filename}"
    else
      h = json
    end

    h.select {|k,v| subkeys.include?(k) }
  end

  def attributes_guess(file, k = 4)
    ids = nearest_feature_ids(file, k)
```

```ruby
    votes = {
      'glasses' => {false => 0, true => 0},
      'facial_hair' => {false => 0, true => 0}
    }

    ids.each do |id|
      resp = self.class.face_class(@ids[id], %w[glasses facial_hair])

      resp.each do |k,v|
        votes[k][v] += 1
      end
    end

    votes
  end
end
```

Now we face the task of making this thing useful. You'll notice that the default value for `attributes_guess` is *K*. We need to find that still.

Cross-validation and finding K

Now we need to actually train and build an optimal model and find our *K*. For that, we're going to first fold our AT&T database into two pieces like so:

```ruby
# test/lib/neighborhood_spec.rb

describe Neighborhood do
  let(:files) { Dir['./public/att_faces/**/*.png'] }

  let(:file_folds) do
    {
      'fold1' => files.each_with_index.select {|f, i| i.even? }.map(&:first),
      'fold2' => files.each_with_index.select {|f, i| i.odd? }.map(&:first)
    }
  end

  let(:neighborhoods) do
    {
      'fold1' => Neighborhood.new(file_folds.fetch('fold1')),
      'fold2' => Neighborhood.new(file_folds.fetch('fold2'))
    }
  end
end
```

Next, we are going to want to build a test for each fold and cross-validate to see what the errors look like. This isn't a unit test at this point because we are doing some experimentation instead. Here is the code we'll use:

```ruby
# test/lib/neighborhood_spec.rb
```

```ruby
describe Neighborhood do
  %w[fold1 fold2].each_with_index do |fold, i|
    other_fold = "fold#{(i + 1) % 2 + 1}"
    it "cross validates #{fold} against #{other_fold}" do
      (1..7).each do |k_exp|
        k = 2 ** k_exp - 1
        errors = 0
        successes = 0

        dist = measure_x_times(2) do
          file_folds.fetch(fold).each do |vf|
            face_class = Neighborhood.face_class(vf, %w[glasses facial_hair])
            actual = neighborhoods.fetch(other_fold).attributes_guess(vf, k)

            face_class.each do |k,v|
              if actual[k][v] > actual[k][!v]
                successes += 1
              else
                errors += 1
              end
            end
          end
        end

        error_rate = errors / (errors + successes).to_f

        avg_time = dist.reduce(Rational(0,1)) do |sum, bm|
          sum += bm.real * Rational(1,2)
        end
        print "#{k}, #{error_rate}, #{avg_time}\n"
      end
    end
  end
end
```

This prints out some useful information in finding our optimal *K*, as you can see in Figure 3-16 (values are shown in Tables 3-4 and 3-5).

Table 3-4. Cross-validation fold #1

K	Error rate	Time to run
1	0.0	1.4284405
2	0.0	0.8799995
4	0.0575	1.3032545
8	0.1775	2.121337
16	0.2525	3.7583905

K	Error rate	Time to run
32	0.255	8.555531
64	0.255	23.3080745

Table 3-5. Cross-validation fold #2

K	Error rate	Time to run
1	0.0	1.4773145
2	0.0	0.9168755
4	0.05	1.3097035
8	0.21	2.1183575
16	0.2475	3.890095
32	0.2475	8.6245775
64	0.2475	23.480187

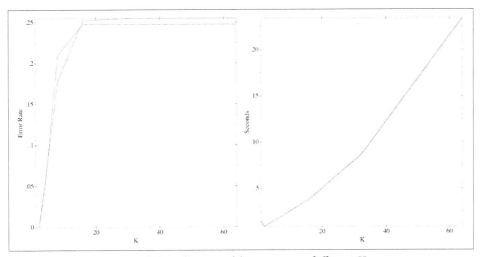

Figure 3-16. Error rate and time (in seconds) to run over different Ks

We now can make a better judgment as to which K to use. Instead of picking the obvious $K = 1$ or $K = 2$, we should use $K = 4$. The reason is because as new data comes in we want to be able to check all four classes and therefore make the model more robust to data changes in the future.

At this time, our code works!

Conclusion

K-Nearest Neighbors is one of the best algorithms for classifying data sets. It is lazy and nonparametric. It also works fairly fast if you're using something like a K-D tree. As you saw in this chapter, KNN is well suited for any type of problem for which you want to model voting or determine whether things are close together.

You also learned about the issues related with KNN, like the curse of dimensionality. When we built our tool to determine whether someone was wearing glasses or had facial hair, we learned quickly that if we looked at all pixels, things would break down, so we had to apply SURF to reduce the dimensions.

Because it follows the Bayes error rate, however, for many problems KNN is a good, suitable tool as a starting point for determining whether you can solve anything at all.

## CHAPTER 4

Naive Bayesian Classification

Remember email several years ago? You probably recall your inbox being full of spam messages ranging from Nigerian princes wanting to pawn off money to pharmaceutical advertisements. It became such a major issue that we spent most of our time filtering spam.

Nowadays, we spend a lot less time filtering spam than we used to, thanks to Gmail and tools like SpamAssassin. Using a method called a Naive Bayesian Classifier, such tools have been able to mitigate the influx of spam to our inboxes. This chapter will explore that topic as well as:

- Bayes' theorem
- What a Naive Bayesian Classifier is and why it's called "naive"
- How to build a spam filter using a Naive Bayesian Classifier

 As noted in Chapter 2, a Naive Bayes Classifier is a supervised and probabalistic learning method. It does well with data in which the inputs are independent from one another. It also prefers problems where the probability of any attribute is greater than zero.

Using Bayes' Theorem to Find Fraudulent Orders

Imagine you're running an online store and lately you've been overrun with fraudulent orders. You estimate that about 10% of all orders coming in are fraudulent. In other words, in 10% of orders, people are stealing from you. Now of course you want to mitigate this by reducing the fraudulent orders, but you are facing a conundrum.

Every month you receive at least 1,000 orders, and if you were to check every single one, you'd spend more money fighting fraud than the fraud was costing you in the first place. Assuming that it takes up to 60 seconds per order to determine whether it's fraudulent or not, and a customer service representative costs around $15 per hour to hire, that totals 200 hours and $3,000 per year.

Another way of approaching this problem would be to construct a probability that an order is over 50% fraudulent. In this case, we'd expect the number of orders we'd have to look at to be much lower. But this is where things become difficult, because the only thing we can determine is the probability that it's fraudulent, which is 10%. Given that piece of information, we'd be back at square one looking at all orders because it's more probable that an order is not fraudulent!

Let's say that we notice that fraudulent orders often use gift cards and multiple promotional codes. Using this knowledge, how would we determine what is fraudulent or not—namely, how would we calculate the probability of fraud given that the purchaser used a gift card?

To answer for that, we first have to talk about *conditional probabilities*.

Conditional Probabilities

Most people understand what we mean by the probability of something happening. For instance, the probability of an order being fraudulent is 10%. That's pretty straightforward. But what about the probability of an order being fraudulent given that it used a gift card? To handle that more complicated case, we need something called a conditional probability, which is defined as follows:

$$P(A \mid B) = \frac{P(A \cap B)}{P(B)}$$

Probability Symbols

Generally speaking, writing $P(E)$ means that you are looking at the probability of a given event. This event can be a lot of different things, including the event that A and B happened, the probability that A or B happened, or the probability of A given B happening in the past. Here we'll cover how you'd notate each of these scenarios:

$A \cap B$ could be called the *and* function, as it is the intersection of A and B. For instance, in Ruby it looks like this:

```ruby
a = [1,2,3]
b = [1,4,5]


a & b #=> [1]
```

$A \cup B$ could be called the or function, as it is both A and B. For instance, in Ruby it looks like the following:

```
a = [1,2,3]
b = [1,4,5]

a | b #=> [1,2,3,4,5]
```

Finally, the probability of *A given B* looks as follows in Ruby:

```
a = [1,2,3]
b = [1,4,5]

total = 6.0

p_a_cap_b = (a & b).length / total
p_b = b.length / total

p_a_given_b = p_a_cap_b / p_b #=> 0.33
```

This definition basically says that the probability of A happening given that B happened is the probability of *A and B* happening divided by the probability of B. Graphically, it looks something like Figure 4-1.

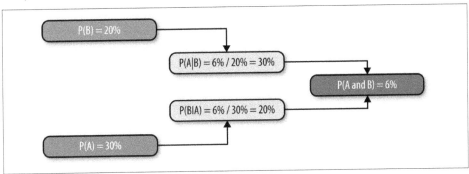

Figure 4-1. This shows how P(A|B) sits between P(A and B) and P(B)

In our fraud example, let's say we want to measure the probability of fraud given that an order used a gift card. This would be $P(Fraud|Giftcard) = \frac{P(Fraud \cap Giftcard)}{P(Giftcard)}$. Now this works if you know the actual probability of *Fraud* and *Giftcard* happening.

At this point, we are up against the problem that we cannot calculate *P(Fraud|Giftcard)* because that is hard to separate out. To solve this problem, we need to use a trick introduced by Bayes.

Inverse Conditional Probability (aka Bayes' Theorem)

In the 1700s, Reverend Thomas Bayes came up with the original research that would become Bayes' theorem. Pierre-Simon Laplace extended Bayes' research to produce the beautiful result we know today. Bayes' theorem is as follows:

$$P(B|A) = \frac{P(A|B)P(B)}{P(A)}$$

This is because of the following:

$$P(B|A) = \frac{\frac{P(A \cap B)P(B)}{P(B)}}{P(A)} = \frac{P(A \cap B)}{P(A)}$$

This is useful in our fraud example because we can effectively back out our result using other information. Using Bayes' theorem, we would now calculate:

$$P(Fraud|Giftcard) = \frac{P(Giftcard|Fraud)P(Fraud)}{P(Giftcard)}$$

Remember that the probability of fraud was 10%. Let's say that the probability of gift card use is 10%, and based on our research the probability of gift card use in a fraudulent order is 60%. So what is the probability that an order is fraudulent given that it uses a gift card?

$$P(Fraud|Giftcard) = \frac{60\% \ 10\%}{10\%} = 60\%$$

The beauty of this is that your work on measuring fraudulent orders is drastically reduced because all you have to look for is the orders with gift cards. Because the total number of orders is 1,000, and 100 of those are fraudulent, we will look at 60 of those fraudulent orders. Out of the remaining 900, 90 used gift cards, which brings the total we need to look at to 150!

At this point, you'll notice we reduced the orders needing fraud review from 1,000 to 40 (i.e., 4% of the total). But can we do better? What about introducing something like people using multiple promo codes or other information?

Naive Bayesian Classifier

We've already solved the problem of finding fraudulent orders given that a gift card was used, but what about the problem of fraudulent orders given the fact that they have gift cards, or multiple promo codes, or other *features*? How would we go about that?

Namely, we want to solve the problem of $P(A \mid B, C) = ?$. For this, we need a bit more information and something called the *chain rule*.

The Chain Rule

If you think back to probability class, you might recall that the probability of A and B happening is the probability of B given A times the probability of A. Mathematically, this looks like $P(A \cap B) = P(B \mid A)P(A)$. This is assuming these events are *not* mutually exclusive. Using something called a *joint probability*, this smaller result transforms into the chain rule.

Joint probabilities are the probability that *all* the events will happen. We denote this by using $\cap$. The generic case of the chain rule is:

$$P(A_1, A_2, ..., A_n) = P(A_1)P(A_2 \mid A_1)P(A_3 \mid A_1, A_2) ... P(A_n \mid A_1, A_2, ..., A_{n-1})$$

This expanded version is useful in trying to solve our problem by feeding lots of information into our Bayesian probability estimates. But there is one problem: this can quickly evolve into a complex calculation using information we don't have, so we make one big assumption and act naive.

Naivety in Bayesian Reasoning

The chain rule is useful for solving potentially inclusive problems, but we don't have the ability to calculate all of those probabilities. For instance, if we were to introduce multiple promos into our fraud example then we'd have the following to calculate:

$$P(Fraud \mid Giftcard, Promos) = \frac{P(Giftcard, Promos \mid Fraud)P(Fraud)}{P(Giftcard, Promos)}$$

Let's ignore the denominator for now, as it doesn't depend on whether the order is fraudulent or not. At this point, we need to focus on finding the calculation for *P(Giftcard, Promos|Fraud)P(Fraud)*. If we apply the chain rule, this is equivalent to *P(Fraud, Giftcard, Promos)*.

You can see this by the following:

$$P(Fraud, Gift, Promo) = P(Fraud)P(Gift, Promo \mid Fraud) = P(Fraud)P(Gift \mid Fraud)P(Promo \mid Fraud, Gift)$$

Now at this point we have a conundrum: how do you measure the probability of a promo code given fraud and gift cards? While this is the correct probability, it really can be difficult to measure—especially with more features coming in. What if we were to be a tad naive and assume that we can get away with independence and just say that we don't care about the interaction between promo codes and gift cards, just the interaction of each independently with fraud?

In that case, our math would be much simpler:

$$P(Fraud, Gift, Promo) = P(Fraud)P(Gift \mid Fraud)P(Promo \mid Fraud)$$

This would be proportional to our numerator. And, to simplify things even more, we can assert that we'll normalize later with some magical Z, which is the sum of all the probabilities of classes. So now our model becomes:

$$P(Fraud \mid Gift, Promo) = \frac{1}{Z}P(Fraud)P(Gift \mid Fraud)P(Promo \mid Fraud)$$

To turn this into a classification problem, we simply determine which input—fraud or not fraud—yields the highest probability. See Table 4-1.

Table 4-1. Probability of gift cards versus promos

	Fraud	Not fraud
Gift card present	60%	10%
Multiple promos used	50%	30%
Probability of class	10%	90%

At this point, you can use this information to determine whether an order is fraudulent based purely on whether it has a gift card present and whether it used multiple promos. The probability that an order is fraudulent given the use of gift cards and multiple promos is 62.5%. While we can't exactly figure out how much savings this gives you in terms of the number of orders you must review, we know that we're using better information and making a better judgment.

There is one problem, though: what happens when the probability of using multiple promos given a fraudulent order is zero? A zero result can happen for several reasons, including that there just isn't enough of a sample size. The way we solve this is by using something called a *pseudocount*.

Pseudocount

There is one big challenge with a Naive Bayesian Classifier, and that is the introduction of new information. For instance, let's say we have a bunch of emails that are classified as spam or ham. We build our probabilities using all of this data, but then something bad happens: a new spammy word, *fuzzbolt*. Nowhere in our data did we see the word *fuzzbolt*, and so when we calculate the probability of spam given the word *fuzzbolt*, we get a probability of zero. This can have a zeroing-out effect that will greatly skew results toward the data we have.

Because a Naive Bayesian Classifier relies on multiplying all of the independent probabilities together to come up with a classification, if any of those probabilities are zero then our probability will be zero.

Take, for instance, the email subject "Fuzzbolt: Prince of Nigeria." Assuming we strip off *of*, we have the data shown in Table 4-2.

Table 4-2. Probability of word given spam or ham

Word	Spam	Ham
Fuzzbolt	0	0
Prince	75%	15%
Nigeria	85%	10%

Now let's assume we want to calculate a score for ham or spam. In both cases, the score would end up being zero because *fuzzbolt* isn't present. At that point, because we have a tie, we'd just go with the more common situation, which is *ham*. This means that we have failed and classified something incorrectly due to one word not being recognized.

There is an easy fix for that: *pseudocount*. When we go about calculating the probability, we add one to the count of the word. So, in other words, everything will end up being word_count + 1. This helps mitigate the zeroing-out effect for now. In the case of our fraud detector, we would add one to each count to ensure that it is never zero.

So in our preceding example, let's say we have 3,000 words. We would give *fuzzbolt* a score of $\frac{1}{3000}$. The other scores would change slightly, but this avoids the zeroing-out problem.

Spam Filter

The canonical machine learning example is building a spam filter. In this section, we will work up a simple spam filter using a Naive Bayesian Classifier and improve it by utilizing a 3-gram tokenization model.

As you have learned before, Naive Bayesian Classifiers can be easily calculated, and operate well under strongly independent conditions. In this example, we will cover the following:

- What the classes look like interacting with each other
- A good data source
- A tokenization model
- An objective to minimize our error
- A way to improve over time

Setup notes

All of the code we're using for this example can be found on Git-Hub (*http://bit.ly/1qwtORP*).

Ruby is constantly changing, so the *README* file is the best place to get up to speed on running the examples.

You will have to make sure libxml is installed.

The Class Diagram

In our example, each email has an object that takes an *.eml* type text file that then tokenizes it into something the SpamTrainer can utilize for incoming email messages. See Figure 4-2 for the class diagram.

Data Source

There are numerous sources of data that we can use, but the best is raw email messages marked as either spam or ham. For our purposes, we can use the CSDMC2010 SPAM corpus, which is available on SourceForge (*http://bit.ly/1qWLKFs*).

This data set has 4,327 total messages, of which 2,949 are ham and 1,378 are spam. For our proof of concept, this should work well enough.

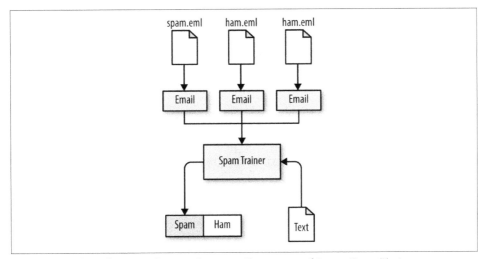

Figure 4-2. Class diagram showing how emails get turned into a SpamTrainer

Email Class

The `Email` class has one responsibility, which is to parse an incoming email message according to the RFC for emails. To handle this, we use the mail gem because there's a lot of nuance in there. In our model, all we're concerned with is subject and body.

The cases we need to handle are HTML messages, plaintext, and multipart. Everything else we'll just ignore.

Building this class using test-driven development, let's go through this step by step.

Starting with the simple plaintext case, we'll copy one of the example training files from our data set under *data/TRAINING/TRAIN_00001.eml* to *./test/fixtures/plain.eml*. This is a plaintext email and will work for our purposes. Note that the split between a message and header in an email is usually denoted by "\r\n\r\n". Along with that header information is generally something like "Subject: A Subject goes here." Using that, we can easily extract our test case, which is:

```
require 'spec_helper'

# test/lib/email_spec.rb

describe Email do
  describe 'plaintext' do
    let(:plain_file) { './test/fixtures/plain.eml' }
    let(:plaintext) { File.read(plain_file) }
    let(:plain_email) { Email.new(plain_file) }

    it 'parses and stores the plain body' do
      body = plaintext.split("\n\n")[1..-1].join("\n\n")
```

```
      plain_email.body.must_equal body
    end

    it 'parses the subject' do
      subject = plaintext.match(/^Subject: (.*)$/)[1]
      plain_email.subject.must_equal subject
    end
  end
end
```

Now instead of relying purely on regular expressions, we want to utilize a gem. We'll use the mail gem, which will handle all of the nitty-gritty details. Making email work for this particular case, we have:

```
require 'forwardable'

# lib/email.rb

class Email
  extend Forwardable

  def_delegators :@mail, :subject

  def initialize(filepath)
    @filepath = filepath
    @mail = Mail.read(filepath)
  end

  def body
    @mail.body.decoded
  end
end
```

You'll notice that we're using `def_delegators` to delegate `subject` to the `@mail` object. This is just for simplicity's sake.

Now that we have captured the case of plaintext, we need to solve the case of HTML. For that, we want to capture only the `inner_text`. Knowing that regular expressions are useless for this, we need yet another gem: Nokogiri. Nokogiri will be able to do this for us easily. But first we need a test case, which looks something like this:

```
# test/lib/email_spec.rb

describe Email do
  describe 'html' do
    let(:html_file) { './test/fixtures/html.eml' }
    let(:html) { File.read(html_file) }
    let(:html_email) { Email.new(html_file) }

    it "parses and stores the html body's inner_text" do
      body = html.split("\n\n")[1..-1].join("\n\n")
      html_email.body.must_equal Nokogiri::HTML.parse(body).inner_text
```

```
      end

    it "stores subject like plaintext does as well" do
      subject = html.match(/^Subject: (.*)$/)[1]
      html_email.subject.must_equal subject
    end
  end
end
```

As mentioned, we're using Nokogiri to calculate the `inner_text`, and we'll have to use it inside of the `Email` class as well. Now the problem is that we also need to detect the `content_type`. So we'll add that in:

```
# lib/email.rb

require 'forwardable'

class Email
  extend Forwardable

  def_delegators :@mail, :subject, :content_type

  def initialize(filepath)
    @filepath = filepath
    @mail = Mail.read(filepath)
  end

  def body
    single_body(@mail.body.decoded, content_type)
  end

  private
  def single_body(body, content_type)
    case content_type
    when 'text/html'
      Nokogiri::HTML.parse(body).inner_text
    when 'text/plain'
      body.to_s
    else
      ''
    end
  end
end
```

At this point, we could add multipart processing as well, but I will leave that as an exercise that you can try out yourself. In the coding repository mentioned earlier in the chapter, you can see the multipart version.

Now we have a working email parser, but we still have to deal with *tokenization*, or what to extract from the body and subject.

Tokenization and Context

As Figure 4-3 shows, there are numerous ways to tokenize text, such as by stems, word frequencies, and words. In the case of spam, we are up against a tough problem because things are more contextual. The phrase *Buy now* sounds spammy, whereas *Buy* and *now* do not. Because we are building a Naive Bayesian Classifier, we are assuming that each individual token is contributing to the spamminess of the email.

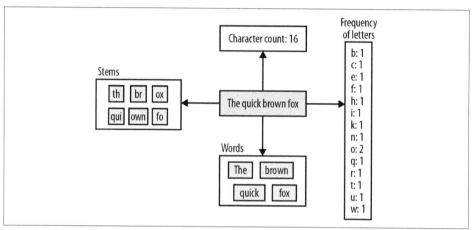

Figure 4-3. There are lots of ways of tokenizing text

The goal of the tokenizer we'll build is to extract words into a stream. Instead of returning an array, we want to yield the token as it happens so that we are keeping a low memory profile. Our tokenizer should also downcase all strings to keep them similar:

```ruby
# test/lib/tokenizer_spec.rb
require 'spec_helper'

describe Tokenizer do
  describe '1-gram tokenization' do
    it 'downcases all words' do
      expectation = %w[this is all caps]
      Tokenizer.tokenize("THIS IS ALL CAPS") do |token|
        token.must_equal expectation.shift
      end
    end
  end

  it 'uses the block if given' do
    expectation = %w[feep foop]
    Tokenizer.tokenize("feep foop") do |token|
      token.must_equal expectation.shift
    end
  end
end
```

```
      end
    end
```

As promised, we do two things in this tokenizer code. First, we lowercase all words. Second, instead of returning an array, we use a block. This is to mitigate memory constraints, as there is no need to build an array and return it. This makes it lazier. To make the subsequent tests work, though, we will have to fill in the skeleton for our tokenizer module like so:

```
# lib/tokenizer.rb

module Tokenizer
  extend self

  def tokenize(string, &block)
    current_word = ''
    return unless string.respond_to?(:scan)
    string.scan(/[a-zA-Z0-9_\u0000]+/).each do |token|
      yield token.downcase
    end
  end
end
```

Now that we have a way of parsing and tokenizing emails, we can move on to the Bayesian portion: the SpamTrainer.

The SpamTrainer

We now need to build the SpamTrainer, which will accomplish three things:

1. Storing training data.
2. Building a Bayesian classifier.
3. Minimizing the false positive rate by testing.

Storing training data

The first step we need to tackle is to store training data from a given set of email messages. In a production environment, you would pick something that has persistence. In our case, we will go with storing everything in one big hash.

Remember that most machine learning algorithms have two steps: training and then computation. Our training step will consist of these substeps:

1. Storing a set of all categories
2. Storing unique word counts for each category
3. Storing the totals for each category

So first we need to capture all of the category names; that test would look something like this:

```
# test/lib/spam_trainer_spec.rb

describe SpamTrainer do
  describe 'initialization' do
    let(:hash_test) do
      {'spam' => './filepath', 'ham' => './another', 'scram' => './another2'}
    end

    it 'allows you to pass in multiple categories' do
      st = SpamTrainer.new(hash_test)
      st.categories.sort.must_equal hash_test.keys.uniq.sort
    end
  end
end
```

The solution is in the following code:

```
# lib/spam_trainer.rb

class SpamTrainer
  def initialize(training_files, n = 1)
    @categories = Set.new

    training_files.each do |tf|
      @categories << tf.first
    end
  end
end
```

You'll notice we're just using a set to capture this for now, as it'll hold on to the unique version of what we need. Our next step is to capture the unique tokens for each email. We are using the special category called _all to capture the count for everything:

```
Subject: One of a kind Money maker! Try it for free!

spam

# test/lib/spam_trainer_spec.rb

describe SpamTrainer do
  let(:training) do
    [['spam','./test/fixtures/plain.eml'], ['ham','./test/fixtures/small.eml']]
  end

  let(:trainer) { SpamTrainer.new(training)}

  it 'initializes counts all at 0 plus an _all category' do
    st = SpamTrainer.new(hash_test)
    %w[_all spam ham scram].each do |cat|
      st.total_for(cat).must_equal 0
```

```
      end
    end
  end
```

To get this to work, we have introduced a new method called `train!`, which will take the training data, iterate over it, and save it into an internal hash. The following is a solution:

```ruby
# lib/spam_trainer.rb

class SpamTrainer
  def initialize(training_files)
    setup!(training_files)
  end

  def setup!(training_files)
    @categories = Set.new

    training_files.each do |tf|
      @categories << tf.first
    end

    @totals = Hash[@categories.map {|c| [c, 0]}]
    @totals.default = 0
    @totals['_all'] = 0

    @training = Hash[@categories.map {|c| [c, Hash.new(0)]}]
  end

  def total_for(category)
    @totals.fetch(category)
  end

  def train!
    @to_train.each do |category, file|
      write(category, file)
    end
    @to_train = []
  end

  def write(category, file)
    email = Email.new(file)

    logger.debug("#{category} #{file}")

    @categories << category
    @training[category] ||= Hash.new(0)

    Tokenizer.unique_tokenizer(email.blob) do |token|
      @training[category][token] += 1
      @totals['_all'] += 1
      @totals[category] += 1
```

```
      end
    end
  end
```

Now we have taken care of the training aspect of our program but really have no clue how well it performs. And it doesn't classify anything. For that, we still need to build our classifier.

Building the Bayesian classifier

To refresh your memory, Bayes' theorem is:

$$P(A_i | B) = \frac{P(B | A_i)P(A_i)}{\Sigma_j P(B | A_j)P(A_j)}$$

But because we're being naive about this, we've distilled it into something much simpler:

Score(Spam, W_1, W_2, ..., W_n) = P(Spam)P(W_1 | Spam)P(W_2 | Spam) ... P(W_n | Spam)

which is then divided by some normalizing constant, *Z*.

Our goal now is to build the methods `score`, `normalized_score`, and `classify`. The `score` method will just be the raw score from the preceding calculation, while `normal ized_score` will fit the range from 0 to 1 (we get this by dividing by the total sum, *Z*).

The `score` method's test is as follows:

```
# test/lib/spam_trainer_spec.rb

describe SpamTrainer do
  describe 'scoring and classification' do
    let (:training) do
      [
        ['spam','./test/fixtures/plain.eml'],
        ['ham','./test/fixtures/plain.eml'],
        ['scram','./test/fixtures/plain.eml']
      ]
    end

    let(:trainer) do
      SpamTrainer.new(training)
    end

    let(:email) { Email.new('./test/fixtures/plain.eml') }

    it 'calculates the probability to be 1/n' do
      scores = trainer.score(email).values
```

```
    assert_in_delta scores.first, scores.last

    scores.each_slice(2) do |slice|
      assert_in_delta slice.first, slice.last
    end
  end
 end
end
```

Because the training data is uniform across the categories, there is no reason for the score to differ across them. To make this work in our `SpamTrainer` object, we will have to fill in the pieces like so:

```
# lib/spam_trainer.rb

class SpamTrainer
  #def initialize
  #def total_for
  #def train!
  #def write

  def score(email)
    train!

    unless email.respond_to?(:blob)
      raise 'Must implement #blob on given object'
    end

    cat_totals = totals

    aggregates = Hash[categories.map do |cat|
      [
        cat,
        Rational(cat_totals.fetch(cat).to_i, cat_totals.fetch("_all").to_i)
      ]
    end]

    Tokenizer.unique_tokenizer(email.blob) do |token|
      categories.each do |cat|
        r = Rational(get(cat, token) + 1, cat_totals.fetch(cat).to_i + 1)
        aggregates[cat] *= r
      end
    end

    aggregates
  end
end
```

This test does the following:

- Trains the model if it's not already trained (the `train!` method handles this).

- For each token of the *blob* of an email we iterate through all categories and calculate the probability of that token being within that category. This calculates the Naive Bayesian score of each without dividing by Z.

Now that we have `score` figured out, we need to build a `normalized_score` that adds up to 1. Testing for this, we have:

```
# test/lib/spam_trainer_spec.rb

describe SpamTrainer do
  it 'calculates the probability to be exactly the same and add up to 1' do
    trainer.normalized_score(email).values.inject(&:+).must_equal 1
    trainer.normalized_score(email).values.first.must_equal Rational(1,3)
  end
end
```

and subsequently on the `SpamTrainer` class we have:

```
# lib/spam_trainer.rb

class SpamTrainer
  #def initialize
  #def total_for
  #def train!
  #def write
  #def score

  def normalized_score(email)
    score = score(email)
    sum = score.values.inject(&:+)

    Hash[score.map do |cat, aggregate|
      [cat, (aggregate / sum).to_f]
    end]
  end
end
```

Calculating a classification

Because we now have a score, we need to calculate a classification for the end user to use. This classification should take the form of an object that returns `guess` and `score`. There is an issue of tie breaking here.

Let's say, for instance, we have a model that has *turkey* and *tofu*. What happens when the scores come back evenly split? Probably the best course of action is to go with which is more popular, whether it be *turkey* or *tofu*. What about the case where the probability is the same? In that case, we can just go with alphabetical order.

When testing for this, we need to introduce a preference order—that is the occurrence of each category. A test for this would be:

```
# test/lib/spam_trainer_spec.rb

describe SpamTrainer do
  describe 'scoring and classification' do
    it 'sets the preference based on how many times a category shows up' do
      expected = trainer.categories.sort_by {|cat| trainer.total_for(cat) }

      trainer.preference.must_equal expected
    end
  end
end
```

Getting this to work is trivial and would look like this:

```
# lib/spam_trainer.rb

class SpamTrainer
  #def initialize
  #def total_for
  #def train!
  #def write
  #def score
  #def normalized_score

  def preference
    categories.sort_by {|cat| total_for(cat) }
  end
end
```

Now that we have preference set up, we can test for our classification being correct. The code to do that is as follows:

```
# test/lib/spam_trainer.rb

describe SpamTrainer do
  describe 'scoring and classification' do
    it 'gives preference to whatever has the most in it' do
      score = trainer.score(email)
      preference = trainer.preference.last
      preference_score = score.fetch(preference)

      expected = SpamTrainer::Classification.new(preference, preference_score)

      trainer.classify(email).must_equal expected
    end
  end
end
```

Getting this to work in code again is simple:

```
# lib/spam_trainer.rb

class SpamTrainer
  Classification = Struct.new(:guess, :score)
```

```
#def initialize
#def total_for
#def train!
#def write
#def score
#def preference
#def normalized_score

def classify(email)
  score = score(email)
  max_score = 0.0
  max_key = preference.last
  score.each do |k,v|
    if v > max_score
      max_key = k
      max_score = v
    elsif v == max_score && preference.index(k) > preference.index(max_key)
      max_key = k
      max_score = v
    else
      # Do nothing
    end
  end
  throw 'error' if max_key.nil?
  Classification.new(max_key, max_score)
end
end
```

Error Minimization Through Cross-Validation

At this point, we need to measure how well our model works. To do so, we need to take the data that we downloaded earlier and do a cross-validation test on it. From there, we need to measure only false positives, and then based on that determine whether we need to fine-tune our model more.

Minimizing false positives

Up until this point, our goal with making models has been to minimize *error*. This error could be easily denoted as the count of misclassifications divided by the total classifications. In most cases, this is exactly what we want, but in a spam filter this isn't what we're optimizing for. Instead, we want to minimize false positives. False positives, also known as Type I errors, are when the model incorrectly predicts a positive when it should have been negative.

In our case, if our model predicts spam when in fact the email isn't, then the user will lose her emails. We want our spam filter to have as few false positives as possible. On the other hand, if our model incorrectly predicts something as ham when it isn't, we don't care as much.

Instead of minimizing the total misclassifications divided by total classifications, we want to minimize spam misclassifications divided by total classifications. We will also measure false negatives, but they are less important because we are trying to reduce spam that enters someone's mailbox, not eliminate it.

To accomplish this, we first need to take some information from our data set, which we'll cover next.

Building the two folds

Inside the spam email training data is a file called *keyfile.label*. It contains information about whether the file is spam or ham. Inside our cross-validation test, we can easily parse the file using the following code:

```
# test/cross_validation_spec.rb

describe 'Cross Validation' do
  def self.parse_emails(keyfile)
    emails = []
    File.open(keyfile, 'rb').each_line do |line|
      label, file = line.split(/\s+/)
      emails << Email.new(filepath, label)
    end
    emails
  end

  def self.label_to_training_data(fold_file)
    training_data = []
    st = SpamTrainer.new([])

    File.open(fold_file, 'rb').each_line do |line|
      label, file = line.split(/\s+/)
      st.write(label, file)
    end

    st
  end

  def self.validate(trainer, set_of_emails)
    correct = 0
    false_positives = 0.0
    false_negatives = 0.0
    confidence = 0.0

    set_of_emails.each do |email|
      classification = trainer.classify(email)
      confidence += classification.score
      if classification.guess == 'spam' && email.category == 'ham'
        false_positives += 1
      elsif classification.guess == 'ham' && email.category == 'spam'
        false_negatives += 1
```

```
      else
        correct += 1
      end
    end

    total = false_positives + false_negatives + correct

    message = <<-EOL
    False Positives: #{false_positives / total}
    False Negatives: #{false_negatives / total}
    Accuracy: #{(false_positives + false_negatives) / total}
    EOL
    message
  end
end
```

Cross-validation and error measuring

From here, we can actually build our cross-validation test, which will read *fold1* and *fold2* and then cross-validate to determine the actual error rate. The test looks something like this:

```
# test/cross_validation_spec.rb
describe 'Cross Validation' do
  describe "Fold1 unigram model" do
    let(:trainer) {
      self.class.label_to_training_data('./test/fixtures/fold1.label')
    }

    let(:emails) {
      self.class.parse_emails('./test/fixtures/fold2.label')
    }

    it "validates fold1 against fold2 with a unigram model" do
      skip(self.class.validate(trainer, emails))
    end
  end

  describe "Fold2 unigram model" do
    let(:trainer) {
      self.class.label_to_training_data('./test/fixtures/fold2.label')
    }

    let(:emails) {
      self.class.parse_emails('./test/fixtures/fold1.label')
    }

    it "validates fold2 against fold1 with a unigram model" do
      skip(self.class.validate(trainer, emails))
    end
  end
end
```

When we run the command ruby test/cross_validation_spec.rb, we get the following results:

```
WARNING: Could not parse (and so ignoring) 'From spamassassin-devel-admin@lists.
sourceforge.net Fri Oct 4 11:07:38 2002'
Parsing emails for ./test/fixtures/fold2.label
WARNING: Could not parse (and so ignoring) 'From quinlan@pathname.com Thu Oct 1
0 12:29:12 2002'
Done parsing emails for ./test/fixtures/fold2.label
Cross Validation::Fold1 unigram model
  validates fold1 against fold2 with a unigram model

        False Positive Rate (Bad): 0.0036985668053629217
        False Negative Rate (not so bad): 0.16458622283865001
        Error Rate: 0.16828478964401294

WARNING: Could not parse (and so ignoring) 'From quinlan@pathname.com Thu Oct 1
0 12:29:12 2002'
Parsing emails for ./test/fixtures/fold1.label
WARNING: Could not parse (and so ignoring) 'From spamassassin-devel-admin@lists.
sourceforge.net Fri Oct 4 11:07:38 2002'
Done parsing emails for ./test/fixtures/fold1.label
Cross Validation::Fold2 unigram model
  validates fold2 against fold1 with a unigram model

        False Positive Rate (Bad): 0.005545286506469501
        False Negative Rate (not so bad): 0.17375231053604437
        Error Rate: 0.17929759704251386
```

You'll notice that the false negative rate (classifying an email as ham when it's actually spam) is much higher than the false positive rate (classifying an email as spam when it's ham). This is because of Bayes' theorem! Let's look at the actual probabilities for ham versus spam in Table 4-3.

Table 4-3. Spam versus ham

Category	Email count	Word count	Probability of email	Probability of word
Spam	1,378	231,472	31.8%	36.3%
Ham	2,949	406,984	68.2	63.7%
Total	4,327	638,456	100%	100%

As you can see, ham is more probable, so we will default to that and more often than not we'll classify something as ham when it might not be. The good thing here, though, is that we have reduced spam by 80% without sacrificing incoming messages.

Conclusion

In this chapter, we have delved into building and understanding a Naive Bayesian Classifier. As you have learned it, this algorithm is well suited for data that can be asserted to be independent. Being a probablistic model, it works well for classifying data into multiple directions given the underlying score. This supervised learning method is useful for fraud detection, spam filtering, and any other problem that has these types of features.

## CHAPTER 5

Hidden Markov Models

Intuition informs much of what we do: for example, it tells us that certain words tend to be a certain part of speech, or that if a user visits a signup page she has a higher probability of becoming a customer. But how would you build a model around intuition?

Hidden Markov Models, which are the subject of this chapter, are versed in finding the underlying state of a given system using observations and an assumption about how those states work. In this chapter, we will first talk about how to track user states given their actions, then explore more about what a Hidden Markov Model is, and finally build a part-of-speech tagger using the Brown Corpus.

Hidden Markov Models can be either supervised or unsupervised and also are called *Markovian* due to their reliance on a Markov Model. They work well where there doesn't need to be a lot of historical information built into the model. They also work well for adding localized context to a classification.

Tracking User Behavior Using State Machines

Have you ever heard of the sales funnel? This is the idea that there are different levels of customer interaction. People will start as prospects and then transition into more engaged states (see Figure 5-1).

Let's say that we have an online store and determine that out of prospects that visit the site, 15% will sign up, and 5% will become customers right away. When the visitor is already a user, he will cancel his account 5% of the time and buy something 15% of the time. If the visitor is a customer, he will cancel his account only 2% of the time

Figure 5-1. The generalized sales funnel, from prospect to customer

and go back to being a regular user 95% of the time instead of continually buying things.

Prospects are "lurkers" who visit the site once or twice but usually don't engage. Users, on the other hand, like to browse and occasionally make purchases. Finally, customers are quite engaged and have bought something but usually don't buy a lot in a short time, and thus go back to being users temporarily.

We could represent the information we have collected in a *transition matrix* (), which shows the probability of going from one state to another.

Table 5-1. Transition probability

	Prospect	User	Customer
Prospect	0.80	0.15	0.05
User	0.05	0.80	0.15
Customer	0.02	0.95	0.03

What the transition probability defines is known as a *state machine* (see Figure 5-2). It also tells us a lot about how our current customers behave. We can determine the conversion rate, attrition rate, and other probabilities. Conversion rate is the probability of a prospect signing up, which would be 20%. This is simply the probability of going from prospect to user plus prospect to customer (15% + 5%). You could also determine the attrition rate by taking the average of 5% and 2%, which is 3.5%.

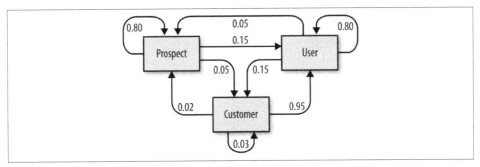

Figure 5-2. A sales funnel state machine with probabilities

This is an uncommon way of displaying user behavior in analytics, because it is too explanatory. But it has one advantage over traditional conversion rate calculations: the ability to look at how a user operates over time. For instance, we could determine the probability of a user being a *prospect* given the last four times he was in fact a *prospect*. This is the probability of being a prospect (say 80%) multiplied by the four times they were a prospect before which were all 80%. The probability that someone keeps viewing the site and never signs up is low, because eventually he might sign up.

But there is also one major problem with this model: there is no way for us to reliably determine these states without asking each user individually. The state is *hidden* from our observation. A user can view the site anonymously.

That is actually fine, as you will soon see. As long as we are able to observe interaction with the site and make a judgment call about the underlying transitions from other sources (think Google Analytics), then we can still solve this problem.

We do this by introducing another level of complexity called *emissions*.

Emissions/Observations of Underlying States

With our preceding example, we don't know when someone goes from being a prospect to a user to a customer. But we are able to observe what a user is doing and what her behavior is. We know that for a given observation there is a probability that she is in a given state.

We can determine the user's underlying state by observing her emitted behaviors. Let's say, for instance, that we have five pages on our website: *Home, Signup, Product, Checkout*, and *Contact Us*. Now, as you might imagine, some of these pages matter to us and others do not. For instance, Signup would most likely mean the prospect becomes a user, and Checkout means the user becomes a customer.

This information gets more interesting because we know the probabilities of states. Let's say we know the emission and state probabilities shown in Table 5-2.

Table 5-2. Emission and state probabilities

Page name	Prospect	User	Customer
Home	0.4	0.3	0.3
Signup	0.1	0.8	0.1
Product	0.1	0.3	0.6
Checkout	0	0.1	0.9
Contact Us	0.7	0.1	0.2

We know the probability of users switching states as well as the probability of the behavior they are emitting given the underlying state. Given this info, what is the probability that a user who has viewed the Home, Signup, and Product pages becomes a customer? Namely, we want to solve the problem depicted in Figure 5-3.

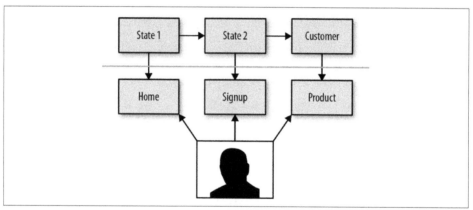

Figure 5-3. You can observe only what your users are doing, but there is a hidden state

To figure this out, we need to determine the probability that a user is in the customer state given all her previous states, or notationally, $P(Customer \mid S_1, S_2)$, as well as the probability of the user viewing the product page given that she was a customer multiplied by the probability of signup given the state, or notationally, $P(Product\_Page \mid Customer) * P(Signup\_Page \mid S_2) * P(Homepage \mid S_1)$. The problem here is that there are more unknowns than knowns.

This finite model is difficult to solve because it involves a lot of calculations. Calculating a problem like $P(Customer \mid S_1, S_2, ..., S_N)$ is complicated. To solve this, we need to introduce the *Markov assumption*.

Emissions and *observations* are used interchangeably in the Hidden Markov Model nomenclature. They are the same thing and refer simply to what a process is emitting or what you can observe.

Simplification through the Markov Assumption

Remember from the Naive Bayesian Classification that each attribute would independently add to the probability of some events. So for spam, the probability would be independently conditional on words or phrases like *Prince* and *Buy now*. In the model that we're building with user behavior, though, we *do* want dependence. Mainly, we want the previous state to be part of the next state's probability. In fact, we would assert that the previous states have a relationship to the user's current state.

In the case of Naive Bayesian Classification, we would make the assumption that the probability of something was independently conditional on other events. So spam was independently conditional on each word in the email.

We can do the same with our current system. We can state that the probability of being in a particular state is primarily based on what happened in the previous state. So instead of $P(Customer \mid S_1, S_2, \ldots, S_n)$, our equation would be $P(Customer \mid S_N)$. But why can we get away with such a gross simplification?

Given a state machine like the one we have just defined, the system infers probabilistically and recursively where you have been in the past. For instance, if a site visitor were in state customer, then you could say that the most probable previous state would be user, and that the most probable state before that would be prospect.

This simplification also has one exciting conclusion, which leads us into our next topic: *Markov chains*.

Using Markov Chains Instead of a Finite State Machine

We have been talking purely about one system, and only one outcome, thus far. But what is powerful about the Markov assumption is that you can model a system as it operates forever. Instead of looking locally at what the process is going to do, we can figure out how the system will always behave. This brings us to the idea of a Markov chain.

Markov chains are exceptional at simulating systems. Queuing theory, finance, weather modeling, and game theory all make heavy use of Markov chains. They are powerful because they represent behaviors in a concise way. We can also quickly determine how we would assume a system to perform given a Markov chain.

Markov chains can analyze and find information out of an underlying process that will operate forever. But that still doesn't solve our fundamental problem, which is that we still need to determine what state a given person is in given his hidden previous state and our own observations. For that, we will need to enhance Markov chains with a hidden aspect.

Hidden Markov Model

We've talked a lot about observation and underlying state transitions, but now we're almost back to where we started. We still need to figure out what a user's state is. To do this, we will use a *Hidden Markov Model*, which comprises these three components:

Evaluation
   How likely is it that a sequence like *Home→Signup→Product→Checkout* will come from our transition and observation of users?

Decoding
   Given this sequence, what does the most likely underlying state sequence look like?

Learning
   Given an observed sequence, what will the user most likely do next?

In the following sections, we will discuss these three elements in detail. First, we'll talk about using the Forward-Backward algorithm to evaluate a sequence of observations. Then we will delve into how to solve the decoding problem with the Viterbi algorithm, which works on a conceptual level. Finally, we'll touch on the idea of learning as an extension of decoding.

Evaluation: Forward-Backward Algorithm

Evaluation is a question of figuring out how probable a given sequence is. This is important in determining how likely it is that your model actually created the sequence that you are modeling. It can also be quite useful for determining, for example, if the sequence *Home→Home* is more probable than *Home→Signup*. We perform the evaluation step by utilizing the Forward-Backward algorithm. This algorithm's goal is to figure out what the probability of a hidden state is subject to the observations.

Mathematical Representation of the Forward-Backward Algorithm

The Forward-Backward algorithm is the probability of an emission happening given its underlying states—that is, $P(e_k|s)$. At first glance, this looks difficult because you would have to compute a lot of probabilities to solve it. If we used the chain rule, this could easily become expansive. Fortunately, we can use a simple trick to solve it instead.

The probability of e_k given an observation sequence is proportional to the joint distribution of e_k and the observations:

$$p(e_k \mid s) \propto p(e_k, s)$$

which we can actually split into two separate pieces using the probability chain rule:

$$p(s_{k+1}, s_{k+2}, ..., s_n \mid e_k, s_1, s_2, ..., s_k)p(e_k, s_1, s_2, ..., s_k)$$

This looks fruitless, but we can actually forget about $x_1, ..., x_k$ in the first probability because the probabilities are *D-Separated*. I won't discuss D-Separation too much, but because we're asserting the Markov assumption in our model we can effectively forget about these variables because they precede what we care about in our probability model:

$$p(e_k \mid s) \propto p(s_{k+1}, s_{k+2}, ..., s_n \mid e_k)p(e_k, s_1, 2_2, ..., s_k)$$

This is the Forward-Backward algorithm!

Graphically, you can imagine this to be a path through this probability space (see Figure 5-4). Given a specific emission at, say, index 2, we could calculate the probability by looking at the forward and backward probabilities.

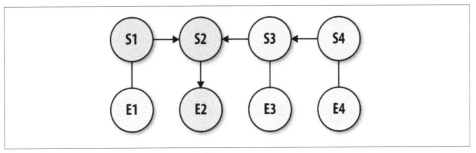

Figure 5-4. Forward-Backward algorithm

The forward term is looking at the joint probability of the hidden state at point k given all the emissions up to that point. The backward term is looking at the conditional probability of emissions from $k+1$ to the end given that hidden point.

Using User Behavior

Using our preceding example of *Home→Signup→Product→Checkout*, let's calculate the probability of that sequence happening inside our model using the Forward-Backward algorithm. First let's set up the problem by building a class called Forward Backward:

```ruby
require 'matrix'
class ForwardBackward
  def initialize
    @observations = ['homepage', 'signup', 'product', 'checkout']

    @states = ['Prospect', 'User', 'Customer']
    @emissions = ['homepage', 'signup', 'product page', 'checkout',
    'contact us']
    @start_probability = [0.8, 0.15, 0.05]

    @transition_probability = Matrix[
      [0.8, 0.15, 0.05],
      [0.05, 0.80, 0.15],
      [0.02, 0.95, 0.03]
    ]

    @emission_probability = Matrix[
      [0.4, 0.3, 0.3], # homepage
      [0.1, 0.8, 0.1], # signup
      [0.1, 0.3, 0.6], # product page
      [0, 0.1, 0.9],   # checkout
      [0.7, 0.1, 0.2]  # contact us
    ]
  end
end
```

Here we are simply importing the information that we had from before—that is, the transition probability matrix as well as the emission probabilities. Next, we need to define our foward step, which is:

```ruby
class ForwardBackward
  # Initialize
  def forward
    forward = []
    f_previous = {}
    @observations.each_with_index do |obs, i|
      f_curr = {}
      @states.each do |state|
        if i.zero?
          prev_f_sum = @start_probability.fetch(state)
        else
          prev_f_sum = @states.reduce(0.0) do |sum, k|
            sum += f_previous.fetch(k, 0.0) * @transition_probabilit.fetch(k).
            fetch(state)
          end
        end
        f_curr[state] = @emission_probability.fetch(state).fetch(obs) *
        prev_f_sum
        forward << f_curr
        f_previous = f_curr
      end
    end
```

```
      p_fwd = @states.reduce(0.0) do |sum, k|
        sum += f_previous.fetch(k) * @transition_probability.fetch(k).fetch
        (@end_state)
      end

      {
        'probability' => p_fwd,
        'sequence' => forward
      }
    end
  end
```

The forward algorithm will go through each state at each observation and multiply them together to get a forward probability of how the state works in this given context. Next, we need to define the backward algorithm, which is:

```
class FowardBackward
  # initialize
  # forward

  def backward
    backward = []
    b_prev = {}

    %w[None].concat(@observations[1..-1].reverse).each_with_index do
    |x_i_plus, i|
      b_curr = {}
      @states.each do |state|
        if i.zero?
          b_curr[state] = @transition_probability.fetch(state).fetch(@end_state)
        else
          b_curr[state] = @states.reduce(0.0) do |sum, k|
            sum += @transition_probability.fetch(state).fetch(k) *
            @emission_probability.fetch(k).fetch(x_i_plus) * b_prev.fetch(k)
          end
        end
      end

      backward.insert(0, b_curr)
      b_prev = b_curr
    end

    p_bkw = @states.reduce(0.0) do |sum, s|
      sum += @start_probability.fetch(s) * @emission_probability.fetch(s).
      fetch(@observations[0]) * b_prev.fetch(s)
    end

    {
      'probability' => p_bkw,
      'sequence' => backward
    }
```

```
      end
    end
```

The backward algorithm works pretty much the same way as the forward one, except that it goes the opposite direction. Next, we need to try both forward and backward and assert that they are the same (otherwise, our algorithm is wrong):

```
class FowardBackward
  # initialize
  # forward
  # backward
  def forward_backward
    size = @observations.length
    fwd, p_fwd = forward.values
    bkwd, p_bkw = backward.values

    # merging the two parts
    posterior = {}
    @states.each do |state|
      posterior[state] = (1..size).map do |i|
        fwd[i][state] * bwkd[i][state] / p_fwd
      end
    end

    return fwd, bkw, posterior
  end
end
```

The beauty of the Forward-Backward algorithm is that it's effectively testing itself as it runs. This is quite exciting. It will also solve the problem of evaluation—remember, that means figuring out how probable a given sequence is likely to be. Next, we'll delve into the decoding problem—that is, figuring out the best sequence of underlying states.

The Decoding Problem through the Viterbi Algorithm

The decoding problem is the easiest to describe. Given a sequence of observations, we want to parse out the best path of states given what we know about them. Mathematically, what we want to find is some specific $\pi^* = \arg \max_\pi P(x, \pi)$, where π is our state vector and x is the observations.

To achieve this, we use the *Viterbi algorithm*. You can think of this as a way of constructing a maximum spanning tree. We are trying to figure out, given our current state, what is the best path to approach next. Similar to any sort of greedy algorithm, the Viterbi algorithm just iterates through all possible next steps and takes it.

Graphically, it would look something like Figure 5-5.

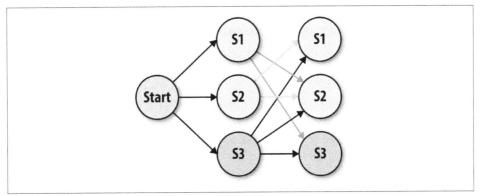

Figure 5-5. A state with high probability will win over time

What we see in this figure is how a state like *S1* will become less relevant over time, while a state of *S3* becomes even more relevant compared to the others. The arrows are shaded to show the probability dampening.

What we are attempting to do with this algorithm is traverse a set of states in the most optimal way. We do this by determining the probability that a state will happen given its emissions as well as the probability that it will transition from the previous state to the current. Then we multiply those two together to get the probability that the sequence will happen. Iterating through the entire sequence, we eventually find our optimal sequence.

The Learning Problem

The learning problem is probably the simplest to actually implement. Given a sequence of states and observations, what is the most likely to happen next? We can do that purely by figuring out the next step in the Viterbi sequence. We figure out the next state by maximizing the next step given the fact there is no emission available yet. But you can figure out the most probable emission from there as well as the most probable state, and that is known as the next optimal state emission combo.

If this way of solving doesn't make sense yet, don't worry: in the next section, we will delve further into using the Viterbi algorithm.

Unfortunately, there isn't any free and easily accessible data available for analyzing user behaviors over time given page views, but there is a similar problem we can solve by using a part-of-speech tagger built purely using a Hidden Markov Model.

Part-of-Speech Tagging with the Brown Corpus

Given the phrase "the quick brown fox," how would you tag its parts of speech? We know that English has parts of speech like determiners, adjectives, and nouns. We would probably tag the words in this phrase as *determiner, adjective, adjective, noun,* respectively. We could fairly easily tag this example because we have a basic understanding of grammar, but how could we train an algorithm to do so?

Well, of course because this is a chapter on Hidden Markov Models, we'll use one to figure out the optimal parts of speech. Knowing what we know about Hidden Markov Models, we can use the Viterbi algorithm to figure out, for a given sequence of words, what is the best tagging sequence. For this section, we will rely on the Brown Corpus, which was the first electronic corpus. It has over a million annotated words with parts of speech in it. The list of tags is long, but rest assured that it contains all the normal tags like adjectives, nouns, and verbs.

The Brown Corpus is set up using a specific kind of annotation. For each sequence of words, you will see something like this:

> Most/ql important/jj of/in all/abn ,/, the/at less/ql developed/vbn countries/nns must/md be/be persuaded/vbn to/to take/vb the/at necessary/jj steps/nns to/to allocate/vb and/cc commit/vb their/pp$ own/jj resources/nns ./.

In this case, *Most* is *ql* which means qualifier, *important* is *jj* (adjective), and on until you reach ./. which is a period tagged as a stop "."

The only thing that this doesn't have is a *START* character at the beginning. Generally speaking, when we're writing Markov models, we want the word at *t* and also the word at *t – 1*. Because *most* is at the front, there is no word before it, so therefore we just use a special name *START* to show that there is a start to this sequence. That way we can measure the probability of going from START to a Qualifier.

Setup Notes

All of the code we're using for this example can be found on GitHub (*http://bit.ly/1qllSE0*).

Ruby is constantly changing, so the *README* file is the best place to find out how to run the examples.

There are no other dependencies for getting this example to run with Ruby.

The Seam of Our Part-of-Speech Tagger: CorpusParser

The *seam* of a part-of-speech tagger is how you feed it data. The most important point is to feed it proper information so that the part-of-speech tagger can utilize and learn from that data. To get started, we need to make some assumptions about how we want it to work. We want to store each transition from a word tag combo in an array of two and then wrap that array in a simple class called `CorpusParser::Tag Word`. Our initial test looks like this:

```
# test/lib/corpus_parser_spec.rb

require 'spec_helper'

describe CorpusParser do
  let (:stream) { "\tSeveral/ap defendants/nns ./.\n" }
  let (:blank) { "\t    \n" }
  it 'will parse a brown corpus line using the standard / notation' do
    cp = CorpusParser.new

    null = CorpusParser::TagWord.new("START", "START")
    several = CorpusParser::TagWord.new("Several", "ap")
    defendants = CorpusParser::TagWord.new("defendants", "nns")
    period = CorpusParser::TagWord.new(".", ".")

    expectations = [
      [null, several],
      [several, defendants],
      [defendants, period]
    ]

    cp.parse(stream) do |ngram|
      ngram.must_equal expectations.shift
    end

    expectations.length.zero?.must_equal true
  end

  it 'does not allow blank lines from happening' do
    cp = CorpusParser.new

    cp.parse(blank) do |ngram|
      raise "Should never happen"
    end
  end
end
```

This code takes two cases that are Brown Corpus–like and checks to make sure they are being parsed properly. The second case is a gut check to make sure it ignores blank lines, as the Brown Corpus is full of them.

Filling in the `CorpusParser` class, we would have something that initially looks like this:

```
# lib/corpus_parser.rb

class CorpusParser
  TagWord = Struct.new(:word, :tag)
  NULL_CHARACTER = "START"
```

```ruby
    STOP = " \n"
    SPLITTER = '/'

    def initialize
      @ngram = 2
    end

    def parse(io)
      ngrams = @ngram.times.map { TagWord.new(NULL_CHARACTER, NULL_CHARACTER) }

      word = ''
      pos = ''
      parse_word = true

      io.each_char do |char|
        if char == "\t" || (word.empty? && STOP.include?(char))
          next
        elsif char == SPLITTER
          parse_word = false
        elsif STOP.include?(char)
          ngrams.shift
          ngrams << TagWord.new(word, pos)

          yield ngrams

          word = ''
          pos = ''
          parse_word = true
        elsif parse_word
          word += char
        else
          pos += char
        end
      end

      unless pos.empty? || word.empty?
        ngrams.shift
        ngrams << TagWord.new(word, pos)
        yield ngrams
      end
    end
  end
end
```

As in the previous chapters, implementing a parser using each_char is generally the most performant way of parsing things in Ruby. Now we can get into the much more interesting part: writing the part-of-speech tagger.

Writing the Part-of-Speech Tagger

We need to be able to do three things with the part-of-speech tagger: take data from the CorpusParser, store it internally so we can calculate probabilities of word tag combos, and do the same for tag transitions. We want this class to be able to tell us how probable a word and tag sequence is, as well as determine from a plaintext sentence what the optimal tag sequence is.

To be able to do that, we need to tackle calculating probabilities first, followed by calculating the probability of a tag sequence with a word sequence. Finally, we'll implement the Viterbi algorithm.

Let's talk about the probability of a tag given its previous tag. Using something called a *maximum likelihood estimate*, we can assert that the probability should equal the count of the two tags together divided by the count of the previous tag. A test for that would look like this:

```ruby
# test/lib/pos_tagger_spec.rb

require 'spec_helper'
require 'stringio'

describe POSTagger do
  let(:stream) { "A/B C/D C/D A/D A/B ./." }

  let(:pos_tagger) {
    pos_tagger = POSTagger.new([StringIO.new(stream)])
    pos_tagger.train!
    pos_tagger
  }

  it 'calculates tag transition probabilities' do
    pos_tagger.tag_probability("Z", "Z").must_equal 0

    # count(previous_tag, current_tag) / count(previous_tag)
    # count D and D happens 2 times, D happens 3 times so 2/3
    pos_tagger.tag_probability("D", "D").must_equal Rational(2,3)
    pos_tagger.tag_probability("START", "B").must_equal 1
    pos_tagger.tag_probability("B", "D").must_equal Rational(1,2)
    pos_tagger.tag_probability(".", "D").must_equal 0
  end
end
```

Remember that the sequence starts with an implied tag called *START*. So here you see the probability of *D* transitioning to *D* is in fact two divided by three, because *D* transitions to *D* three times but *D* shows up three times in that sequence. To make this work, we would have to write the following in our POSTagger class:

```ruby
# lib/pos_tagger.rb

class POSTagger
  def initialize(data_io = [])
    @corpus_parser = CorpusParser.new
    @data_io = data_io
```

```ruby
    @trained = false
  end

  def train!
    unless @trained
      @tags = Set.new(["START"])
      @tag_combos = Hash.new(0)
      @tag_frequencies = Hash.new(0)
      @word_tag_combos = Hash.new(0)

      @data_io.each do |io|
        io.each_line do |line|
          @corpus_parser.parse(line) do |ngram|
            write(ngram)
          end
        end
      end
      @trained = true
    end
  end

  def write(ngram)
    if ngram.first.tag == 'START'
      @tag_frequencies['START'] += 1
      @word_tag_combos['START/START'] += 1
    end

    @tags << ngram.last.tag

    @tag_frequencies[ngram.last.tag] += 1
    @word_tag_combos[[ngram.last.word, ngram.last.tag].join("/")] += 1
    @tag_combos[[ngram.first.tag, ngram.last.tag].join("/")] += 1
  end

  # Maximum likelihood estimate
  # count(previous_tag, current_tag) / count(previous_tag)
  def tag_probability(previous_tag, current_tag)
    denom = @tag_frequencies[previous_tag]

    if denom.zero?
      0
    else
      @tag_combos["#{previous_tag}/#{current_tag}"] / denom.to_f
    end
  end
end
```

You'll notice that we're doing a bit of error handling for the case when zeros happen, because we will throw a divide-by-zero error. Next, we need to address the probability of word tag combinations, which we can do by introducing the following to our existing test:

```
# test/lib/pos_tagger_spec.rb

describe POSTagger do
  let(:stream) { "A/B C/D C/D A/D A/B ./." }
  # Maximum Liklihood estimate
  # count (word and tag) / count(tag)
  it 'calculates the probability of a word given a tag' do
    pos_tagger.word_tag_probability("Z", "Z").must_equal 0

    # A and B happens 2 times, count of b happens twice therefore 100%
    pos_tagger.word_tag_probability("A", "B").must_equal 1

    # A and D happens 1 time, count of D happens 3 times so 1/3
    pos_tagger.word_tag_probability("A", "D").must_equal Rational(1,3)

    # START and START happens 1, time, count of start happens 1 so 1
    pos_tagger.word_tag_probability("START", "START").must_equal 1

    pos_tagger.word_tag_probability(".", ".").must_equal 1
  end
end
```

To make this work in the POSTagger, we need to write the following:

```
# lib/pos_tagger.rb

class POSTagger
  # initialize
  # train!
  # write
  # tag_probability

  # Maximum likelihood estimate
  # count (word and tag) / count(tag)
  def word_tag_probability(word, tag)
    denom = @tag_frequencies[tag]

    if denom.zero?
      0
    else
      @word_tag_combos["#{word}/#{tag}"] / denom.to_f
    end
  end
end
```

Now that we have those two things—word_tag_probability and tag_probability —we can answer the question: given a word and tag sequence, how probable is it? That is the probability of the current tag given the previous tag, multiplied by the word given the tag. In a test, it looks like this:

```
# test/lib/pos_tagger.rb

describe POSTagger do
```

```
it 'calculates probability of sequence of words and tags' do
  words = %w[START A C A A .]
  tags = %w[START B D D B .]
  tagger = pos_tagger

  tag_probabilities = [
    tagger.tag_probability("B", "D"),
    tagger.tag_probability("D", "D"),
    tagger.tag_probability("D", "B"),
    tagger.tag_probability("B", ".")
  ].reduce(&:*)

  word_probabilities = [
    tagger.word_tag_probability("A", "B"), # 1
    tagger.word_tag_probability("C", "D"),
    tagger.word_tag_probability("A", "D"),
    tagger.word_tag_probability("A", "B"), # 1
  ].reduce(&:*)

  expected = word_probabilities * tag_probabilities

  pos_tagger.probability_of_word_tag(words, tags).must_equal expected
end
end
```

So basically we are calculating word tag probabilities multiplied by the probability of
tag transitions. We can easily implement this in the POSTagger using the following:

```
# lib/pos_tagger.rb

class POSTagger
  # initialize
  # train!
  # write
  # tag_probability
  # word_tag_probability

  def probability_of_word_tag(word_sequence, tag_sequence)
    if word_sequence.length != tag_sequence.length
      raise 'The word and tags must be the same length!'
    end
    # word_sequence %w[START I want to race .]
    # Tag sequence %w[START PRO V TO V .]

    length = word_sequence.length

    probability = Rational(1,1)

    (1...length).each do |i|
      probability *= (
        tag_probability(tag_sequence[i - 1], tag_sequence[i]) *
        word_tag_probability(word_sequence[i], tag_sequence[i])
      )
```

```
        end

      probability
    end
  end
```

Now we can figure out how probable a given word and tag sequence is. But it would be better if we were able to determine, given a sentence and training data, what the optimal sequence of tags is. For that, we need to write this simple test:

```
# test/lib/pos_tagger_spec.rb

describe POSTagger do
  describe 'viterbi' do
    let(:training) { "I/PRO want/V to/TO race/V ./. I/PRO like/V cats/N ./." }
    let(:sentence) { 'I want to race.' }
    let(:pos_tagger) {
      pos_tagger = POSTagger.new([StringIO.new(training)])
      pos_tagger.train!
      pos_tagger
    }

    it 'will calculate the best viterbi sequence for I want to race' do
      pos_tagger.viterbi(sentence).must_equal %w[START PRO V TO V .]
    end
  end
end
```

This test takes a bit more to implement because the Viterbi algorithm is somewhat involved. So let's go through this step by step. The first problem is that our method accepts a string, not a sequence of tokens. We need to split by whitespace and treat stop characters as their own word. So to do that, we write the following to set up the Viterbi algorithm:

```
# lib/pos_tagger.rb

class POSTagger
  # initialize
  # train!
  # write
  # tag_probability
  # word_tag_probability

  def viterbi(sentence)
    parts = sentence.gsub(/[\.\?!]/) {|a| " #{a}" }.split(/\s+/)
  end
end
```

The Viterbi algorithm is an *iterative* algorithm, meaning at each step it figures out where it should go next based on the previous answer. So we will need to *memoize* the previous probabilities as well as keep the best tag. We can initialize and figure out what the best tag is as follows:

```ruby
# lib/pos_tagger.rb

class POSTagger
  # initialize
  # train!
  # write
  # tag_probability
  # word_tag_probability

  def viterbi(sentence)
    # parts

    last_viterbi = {}
    backpointers = ["START"]

    @tags.each do |tag|
      if tag == 'START'
        next
      else
        probability = (
          tag_probability("START", tag) *
          word_tag_probability(parts.first, tag)
        )

        if probability > 0
          last_viterbi[tag] = probability
        end
      end
    end

    backpointers << (
      last_viterbi.max_by {|k,v| v} ||
      @tag_frequencies.max_by {|k,v| v}
    ).first
  end
end
```

At this point, `last_viterbi` has only one option, which is {"PRO" ⇒ 1.0}. That is because the probability of transitioning from START to anything else is zero. Likewise, backpointers will have START and PRO in it. So, now that we've set up our initial step, all we need to do is iterate through the rest:

```ruby
# lib/pos_tagger.rb

class POSTagger
  # initialize
  # train!
  # write
  # tag_probability
  # word_tag_probability

  def viterbi(sentence)
```

```ruby
    # parts
    # initialization


parts[1..-1].each do |part|
  viterbi = {}
  @tags.each do |tag|
    next if tag == 'START'
    break if last_viterbi.empty?

    best_previous = last_viterbi.max_by do |prev_tag, probability|
      (
        probability *
        tag_probability(prev_tag, tag) *
        word_tag_probability(part, tag)
      )
    end

    best_tag = best_previous.first

    probability = (
      last_viterbi[best_tag] *
      tag_probability(best_tag, tag) *
      word_tag_probability(part, tag)
    )

    if probability > 0
      viterbi[tag] = probability
    end
  end


  last_viterbi = viterbi

  backpointers << (
    last_viterbi.max_by{|k,v| v} ||
    @tag_frequencies.max_by{|k,v| v }
  ).first
end
backpointers
  end
end
```

What we are doing is storing only relevant information, and if there's a case where last_viterbi is empty, we'll use @tag_frequencies instead. That case really only happens when we have pruned too far. But this approach is much faster than storing all of the information in memory.

At this point, things should work! But how well?

Cross-Validating to Get Confidence in the Model

At this stage, it is prudent to write a cross-validation test. This is using a naive model, but we want to see at least 20% accuracy. So let's write this into a tenfold cross-validation spec. Instead of requiring that this model be within a range of confidence, we will just display the error rate to the user. When I ran the test on my machine, I got around 30% error rate. We will talk about how to improve this, but for our purposes, it's good given that it looks at only two probabilities:

```ruby
# test/cross_validation_spec.rb

require 'spec_helper'

describe "Cross Validation" do
  let(:files) { Dir['./data/brown/c***'] }

  FOLDS = 10

  FOLDS.times do |i|
    let(:validation_indexes) do
      splits = files.length / FOLDS
      ((i * splits)..((i + 1) * splits)).to_a
    end

    let(:training_indexes) do
      files.length.times.to_a - validation_indexes
    end

    let(:validation_files) do
      files.select.with_index {|f, i| validation_indexes.include?(i) }
    end

    let(:training_files) do
      files.select.with_index {|f, i| training_indexes.include?(i) }
    end

    it "cross validates with a low error for fold #{i}" do
      pos_tagger = POSTagger.from_filepaths(training_files, true)
      misses = 0
      successes = 0

      validation_files.each do |vf|
        File.open(vf, 'rb').each_line do |l|
          if l =~ /\A\s+\z/
            next
          else
            words = []
            parts_of_speech = ['START']
            l.strip.split(/\s+/).each do |ppp|
              z = ppp.split('/')
              words << z.first
```

```
            parts_of_speech << z.last
          end

          tag_seq = pos_tagger.viterbi(words.join(' '))
          misses += tag_seq.zip(parts_of_speech).count {|k,v| k != v }
          successes += tag_seq.zip(parts_of_speech).count {|k,v| k == v }
        end
      end
      puts Rational(misses, successes + misses).to_f
    end
    skip("Error rate was #{misses / (successes + misses).to_f}")
  end
 end
end
```

This will yield around a 20–30% error rate, which realistically isn't accurate. Part of the problem, though, is that the Brown Corpus makes a lot of distinction between tags, so the error rate would be much lower if you didn't care about, say, possessive pronouns versus regular pronouns.

How to Make This Model Better

As with all of our coding examples, the best way to improve this model is to first determine how well it works and to iterate. One quick way to make this model operate better would be to look back more than one word at a time. So instead of the probability of a tag given the previous tag, you'd find the probability of a tag given the previous two tags. You could do that by modifying the corpus tagger.

But the example does work well and is simple to make!

Conclusion

Hidden Markov Models are some of the most interesting models when it comes to determining underlying data from a system given some observable data. For example, you can determine the real state of a user, find the underlying tag of a word, or even follow musical scores.

In this chapter, you learned about how state machines can be generalized into Markov chains, which then can be used to model system behavior forever. We also added a hidden component to determine underlying state of a model given emissions that we can easily observe. You learned that the three stages of using Hidden Markov Models are evaluation, decoding, and learning, as well as how to approach solving those problems. Finally, we tagged parts of speech using the Brown Corpus and the Viterbi algorithm.

## CHAPTER 6

Support Vector Machines

What makes a user loyal or not? Loyalty in commerce generally has to do with users returning to buy things consistently over time. But how do you actually measure the deciding factor between loyal and disloyal?

In this chapter, we'll set out to solve that problem conceptually by utilizing Support Vector Machines. This algorithm utilizes many feature objects while yielding a deciding line between one class and the other (e.g., loyal and disloyal). We'll finish up with a worked-out example about attaching sentiment to movie reviews.

Solving the Loyalty Mapping Problem

Our online store has two sets of customers, loyal and disloyal. The loyal customers return to the site consistently and buy from the company, while the disloyal customers are either window shoppers or spendthrifts who don't care about the company. Our goal is to determine what makes a customer loyal and disloyal with respect to the number of orders they place and their average order size.

Let's imagine our data looks something like Figure 6-1.

As we're approaching this problem for the first time, there are many ways we could build something to decide whether users are loyal or disloyal. We could utilize a K-Nearest Neighbors classification program (as described in Chapter 3), which effectively clusters things together around a centroid (see Figure 6-2).

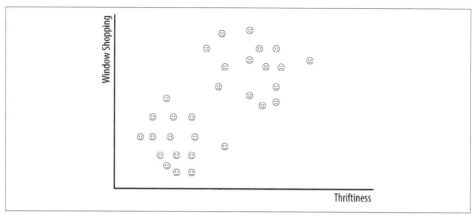

Figure 6-1. There's a discernible difference between loyal and disloyal customers

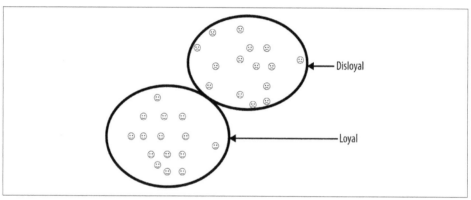

Figure 6-2. Using clustering, we'd build a classification like this

But this is not exactly what we want. We don't want to know what the average loyal or disloyal user looks like; rather, we're trying to find the *decision boundary* between the two. This decision boundary is just a line drawn between the two classes of data. Unfortunately, though, this process isn't as easy as it sounds because there is an infinite number of decision boundaries we can draw.

Luckily for us, there is an algorithm that can help with this problem: Support Vector Machine (SVM). SVM was originally introduced by Vladimir Vapnik in the 1980s as a way of classifying data. The modern interpretation (*http://bit.ly/1pgVqGQ*), introduced in 1995, is less stringent than the first. The original motivation for SVM was to help solve a two-group classification problem. These types of problems can either be boolean (true, false), ids (3,4), or negative positive (1,–1). What makes SVM so special is that it operates well in a high number of dimensions, and avoids the curse of dimensionality. It is also generally fast to compute.

Instead of picking an arbitrary line between two sets of data, the algorithm maximizes the distance between them (see Figure 6-3). So, for instance, in our loyal versus disloyal problem, we would be able to determine the best decision boundary between the two classes. Knowing that decision boundary, we could then answer the question of what *makes* a loyal customer versus what doesn't.

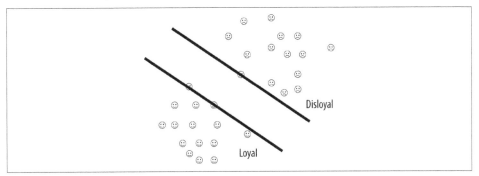

Figure 6-3. Using SVM, we separate two sets of data using a margin

Derivation of SVM

Conceptually, we understand that SVM maximizes the distance between two sets, but *how* does it actually do it?

Our goal is to solve for w for the function $wx - b = 0$ (Figure 6-4). This function could also be rewritten as $b = \sum_{i=1}^{n} w_i x_i$, where x_i is the value at that dimension and w_i is yet to be determined. These equations define a hyperplane or flat surface in an n-dimensional space. *Hyperplane* is just a fancy word for n-dimensional lines between things. What is most important to realize here is that we're drawing a flat surface between two sets and determining the distance between the most outlying data points.

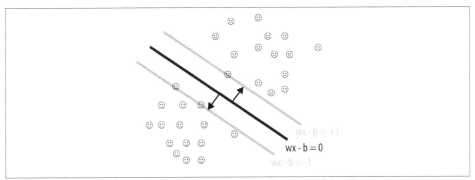

Figure 6-4. Using $wx - b = 0$ we define the hyperplane that separates the two data classes

But this is just an arbitrary space between two classes of data. We want to find the maximum separation of both sets. For that, we will need to define two more hyperplanes: one above and one below the existing one. In our case, we can define them as *wx + b = 1* for the hyperplane above, and *wx + b = –1* for the one below. At this point, we don't know any actual data, but we have a margin above and a margin below.

Now that we have three hyperplanes defined, we want to maximize the margin between the upper and lower hyperplane. We do this through geometry. We have two parallel lines that we need to find the general distance between. The only way of determining this is by finding a hyperplane that moves perpendicular to all the hyperplanes. In our case, the perpendicular segment between the upper and lower hyperplanes happens to be $\frac{2}{||w||}$. Our original goal was to maximize the margin, but we can simplify that by stating that our goal is to *minimize $||w||$*, which is the Euclidean distance between the two hyperplanes.

This approach has many benefits, one of which is that $||w|| = \sqrt{ww}$ (meaning that this is a convex function). Convex functions can be solved quickly thanks to many available algorithms. However, there's an even better option: we can redefine our function to be $\frac{1}{2}||w||^2$, which is called a *quadratic program*. Using the *Karush-Kuhn Tucker* conditions, we can easily solve this problem.

Now we have a way of maximizing the margin between two data sets. Not only that, it is a simple quadratic program and can be quickly computed. But there still is one problem, and that is what happens when there is nonlinear data.

Nonlinear Data

You have probably noticed that all of our examples are linear. Most data, however, isn't linear and has many dimensions. We would like to be able to transform it into something that is more robust, and nonlinear. We can do this with SVM using something called the kernel trick. Effectively, it converts a linear aspect of the model into a nonlinear one, and handles many issues related to nonlinear data.

The Kernel Trick

Imagine you are given a data set that cannot be separated using any linear decision boundaries (Figure 6-5).

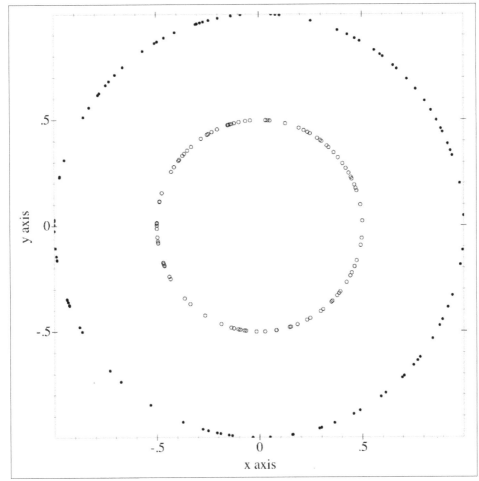

Figure 6-5. A circle within a circle cannot be separated by a line

You'll notice that there is no way of drawing a single line to separate this data. Instead, we would need something nonlinear, like a circle, to do so. Using any sort of linear decision boundary, we couldn't separate the classes here into two different circles. Luckily, there is a trick we can use to overcome this! The *kernel trick* simply transforms data from one type to another. For instance, instead of looking at this circle in a two-dimensional space, what if we were to transform $< x,y >$ to $< x^2, \sqrt{2}xy, y^2 >$? We'd get the result shown in Figure 6-6.

This is the kernel trick in a nutshell. Basically, it takes data that is of one dimension and projects it into more dimensions so that we can use lines to separate it. In this case, we are using a *polynomial kernel*.

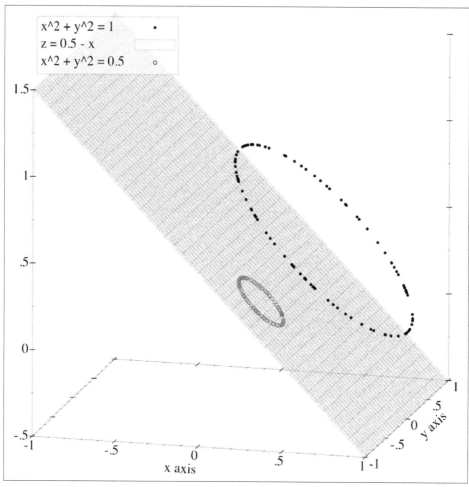

Figure 6-6. This is a different way of looking at the same data

Mathematically speaking, the kernel trick takes a linear x and turns it into $\phi(x)$ or a function of x that better suits the data. There are a couple of points to consider with the kernel trick, however:

- $\phi(x_i)\dot\phi(x_j)$ being calculated many times might take a long time.
- ϕ itself might be a complicated function that is hard to compute.
- If the training data is extensive, then in general the kernel trick will be slow to compute.

So instead of converting all of our xs into $\phi(x)$, perhaps we could try something different, like $k(x_i, x_j) = \phi(x_j) * \phi(x_i)$. Instead of just mapping the original x to a new function, we map the *dot product* of $\phi(x)$.

We need something that is cheap to compute as well. The good news is that such a thing actually exists! It is called a *kernel function*. This type of function has the inner dot product already calculated, so it avoids that step, and it is optimized for speed.

The following kernel functions also have the beneficial property of $K(x,y) = \langle\phi(x),\phi(y)\rangle$:

- Homogenous polynomial
- Heterogenous polynomial
- Radial basis function

Homogenous polynomial

The simplest case of a kernel function is a homogenous polynomial:

$$K\left(x_i, x_j\right) = \left(x_i^T x_j\right)^d$$

where d is the degree of the polynomial and can take any number above 0. This function is used extensively in handwriting detection because of its performance and ease of use.

A polynomial kernel is useful because it uses similarity as well as combinations of data. For instance, let's look at the case of $d = 2$:

$$K(x, y) = \left(\Sigma_{i=1}^n x_i y_i\right)^2 = \Sigma_{i=1}^n x_i^2 y_i^2 + \Sigma_{i=2}^n \Sigma_{j=1}^{i-1} \sqrt{2} x_i y_i \sqrt{2} x_j x_i$$

While that looks like gobbledygook, there's something very interesting going on here. There is the interaction of $x_i^2 y_i^2$, which is to be expected, but also the combinations of $x_i y_i * x_j y_j$. This is very useful for the case where certain dimensions should be grouped together.

Note that Figure 6-6 showed a homogenous polynomial; it uses the degree of 2, which in most cases works best.

Heterogenous polynomial

The heterogeneous polynomial is like the homogenous one except it introduces a non-negative constant, c, which is strictly greater than 0.

This looks like the following:

$$K\left(x_i, x_j\right) = \left(x_i^T x_j + c\right)^d$$

This added constant c increases the relevance of higher-order features instead of the lower ones.

Radial basis functions

A radial basis function (RBF), which is used more often than the aforementioned two polynomials because of its performance in higher dimensions, takes the form of:

$$K\left(x_i, x_j\right) = exp\left(- \frac{\|x_i - x_j\|_2^2}{2 * \sigma^2} \right)$$

The numerator is the squared Euclidean distance. σ is a free parameter.

Unfortunately, there isn't a neat way of visualizing the radial basis function. Of note here is that the kernel will effectively create an infinite number of new dimensions instead of—as is the case with the homogenous polynomial—creating only one more dimension. This is actually a huge feature for RBFs because you overcome the issues related to the curse of dimensionality just by using it.

When should you use each kernel?

The decision of when to use a heterogeneous polynomial versus an *RBF* is a tricky one. Many times, libraries that work with SVM utilize *RBFs* as a default. But this isn't a great reason to use something. According to one paper (*http://bit.ly/1DbtYEV*), these kernels can regularize your data and basically add a low pass filter on it.

Conceptually, a polynomial kernel of degree 2 will take data from two dimensions to three, trying to fit the flattest surface to that. Oftentimes, though, RBFs and polynomial kernels are deemed necessary when in fact they are overfitting the data, so use them with caution.

Soft Margins

There is a challenge with what we have discussed so far, which is that data sets need to be *purely* separable. Imagine the case where our customer is not really loyal but *appears* loyal (see Figure 6-7).

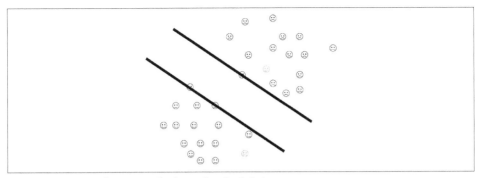

Figure 6-7. Errors happen, which is why slack is important

In this figure, our disloyal customer is in the loyal camp. The data is still linearly separable, but there are a few errors. Instead of trying to find the perfect kernel function, we should really just ignore those errors. When Vladimir Vapnik originally introduced SVM, the assumption was that data was separable using either a linear function or some kind of kernel function. But in most cases, data isn't that pretty, so we'll need to take some steps to optimize it:

1. Optimize with slack.
2. Introduce a new parameter called C.

Optimizing with slack

The data in all of our preceding examples looks pretty, but if we were to optimize something that wasn't purely separated, then our pretty data would break down quickly. There is an elegant way to optimize such data, fortunately: by introducing a *slack variable*.

Instead of the optimization problem purely minimizing $\frac{1}{2}||w||^2$, now we'll introduce the variables ξ_i, which will trade off the error. These *slack variables* are really just margin errors. We want to minimize margin errors as well, so we can add this into our optimization problem as $\frac{1}{2}||w||^2 + \sum_{i=1}^{n} \xi_i$. Effectively, we are adding error parameters to the minimization problem.

Trading off margin maximization with slack variable minimization using C

In the preceding minimization problem, you'll notice that we are weighting the maximization of margins, or $\frac{1}{2}||w||^2$, equal with our sum of slack variables or margin errors. As you know, machine learning is full of trade-offs, so this approach might work and it might not. What Vapnik did instead was to introduce a complexity parameter that could weight the slack variables. This parameter, which is user defined, weights the slack variables against the original margin maximization problem.

Our minimization function is now:

$$\frac{1}{2}||w||^2 + C\left(\sum_{i=1}^{n} \xi_i\right)$$

Practically, this complexity parameter is positive, and can generally be found through cross-validation. We will dig deeper into how to find this complexity parameter in the next section, where we will build a sentiment analyzer using SVM!

Using SVM to Determine Sentiment

Imagine that you want to attach sentiment to a string of words. How would you go about doing that? Language is full of contextual clues, sarcasm, and lots of complexity. The sentiment of a sentence like "Let's get stupid" is ambiguous because it could be either positive or negative.

In this section, we'll build a sentiment analyzer that determines the sentiment of movie reviews. We'll first talk about what this tool will look like conceptually in a class diagram. Then, after identifying the pieces of the tool, we will build a Corpus class, a CorpusSet class, and finally the SentimentClassifier class. The Corpus and CorpusSet classes involve transforming the text into numerical information. SentimentClassifier is where we will then use the SVM algorithm to build this sentiment analyzer.

Setup Notes

All of the code we are using for this example can be found on GitHub (*http://bit.ly/1tXhSZx*).

Ruby is constantly changing, so the *README* file is the best place to get up to speed on running the examples.

There are no additional dependencies beyond a running Ruby version to run this example.

The Class Diagram

Our tool will take a set of training words and sentences that are either negative or positive. Using these sentences we will then build up a corpus of information. In the Corpus class we have either negative- or positive-leaning text, delimited by stop symbols (punctuation symbols like !, ?, or .). Once we have built up a corpus of negative- or positive-leaning text, we need to combine it into a CorpusSet class. This merely puts two or more CorpusSets together into one object.

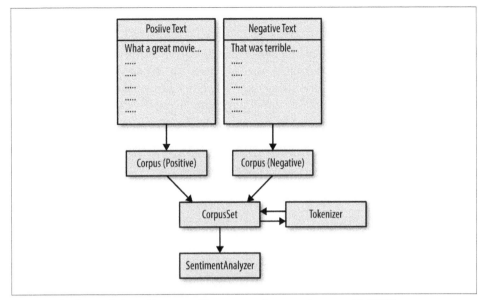

Figure 6-8. General class diagram of how to analyze sentiment with SVM

From there, the `CorpusSet` class will then be used by the `SentimentClassifier` model to build a sentiment analysis guess for use in the future. Figure 6-8 shows the class diagram for this example.

What Do Corpus and Corpora Mean?

Corpus, like *corpse*, means a body, but in this case it's a body of writings. This word is used heavily in the natural language processing community to signal a big group of previous writings that can be used to infer knowledge. In our example, we are using *corpus* to refer to a body of writings around a certain sentiment.

Corpora is simply the plural of corpus.

Corpus Class

Our `Corpus` class will handle the following:

- Tokenizing text
- Sentiment leaning, whether `:negative` or `:positive`
- Mapping from sentiment leaning to a numerical value
- Returning a unique set of words from the corpus

Tokenization of text

As you learned in Chapter 4, there are many different ways of tokenizing text, such as extracting out stems, frequency of letters, emoticons, and words (see Figure 6-9). For our purposes, we will just tokenize words. These are defined as strings between nonalpha characters. So out of a string like "The quick brown fox." we would extract *the, quick, brown, fox*. We don't care about punctuation and we want to be able to skip Unicode spaces and nonwords.

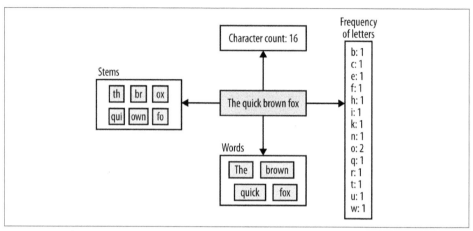

Figure 6-9. There are many ways to tokenize sentences and text

A test of our tokenization would look something like this:

```
# test/lib/corpus_spec.rb

require 'spec_helper'
require 'stringio'

describe Corpus do
  describe "tokenize" do
    it "downcases all the word tokens" do
      Corpus.tokenize("Quick Brown Fox").must_equal %w[quick brown fox]
    end

    it "ignores all stop symbols" do
      Corpus.tokenize("\"'hello!?!?!.'\"  ").must_equal %w[hello]
    end

    it "ignores the unicode space" do
      Corpus.tokenize("hello\u00A0bob").must_equal %w[hello bob]
    end
  end
end
```

From here, we can build our class method `::tokenize` to actually work given our test cases:

```
# lib/corpus.rb

class Corpus
  def self.tokenize(string)
    string.downcase.gsub(/['"\.\?\!]/, '').split(/[[:space:]]/)
  end
end
```

 We are using [[:space]], which in Ruby means that we will split by Unicode and non-Unicode spaces.

While you could spend a lot of time optimizing this tokenization step, this works well enough for our purposes. In machine learning, getting more data points often beats optimizing the minute details.

Sentiment leaning, :positive or :negative

For each `Corpus`, we need to attach a certain leaning, whether it's positive or negative. In most cases, we could attach just an arbitrary number, like –1 or 1, but because those are arbitrary, we should use something more specific. Instead, let's use the symbols `:positive` and `:negative`.

All we care about is whether the symbol comes back, so a test for that would look as follows:

```
# test/lib/corpus_spec.rb

describe Corpus do
  let(:positive) { StringIO.new('loved movie!! loved') }
  let(:positive_corpus) { Corpus.new(positive, :positive) }

  it 'consumes a positive training set' do
    positive_corpus.sentiment.must_equal :positive
  end
end
```

To make this work, let's build a skeleton class that takes in `file` and `sentiment` and makes an `attr_reader` for `:sentiment`:

```
# lib/corpus.rb

class Corpus
  # tokenize
```

```
  attr_reader :sentiment
  def initialize(file, sentiment)
    @file = file
    @sentiment = sentiment
  end
end
```

That was a simple fix. Notice that we have also introduced a file for the Corpus, which will point at our training files.

Sentiment codes for :positive and :negative

As you might imagine, there is an issue with our current code. You could pass anything in as a sentiment and it's not mapping to any numerical sentiment, whether –1 or 1. That's really useless for our purposes if we want to use the SVM algorithm. Instead, we should test for the two cases that are correct and one that is incorrect:

```
# test/lib/corpus_spec.rb

describe Corpus do
  it 'defines a sentiment_code of 1 for positive' do
    Corpus.new(StringIO.new(''), :positive).sentiment_code.must_equal 1
  end

  it 'defines a sentiment_code of 1 for positive' do
    Corpus.new(StringIO.new(''), :negative).sentiment_code.must_equal -1
  end
end
```

This is a simplistic mapping we will use for our SVM to train against. To achieve this, we just write the following:

```
# lib/corpus.rb

class Corpus
  # initialize
  # tokenize

  attr_reader :sentiment

  def sentiment_code
    {
      :positive => 1,
      :negative => -1
    }.fetch(@sentiment)
  end
end
```

Return a Unique Set of Words from the Corpus

Now we have one last step, which is to return the unique set of words from this training file. The goal here is to return words that are located in the corpus so that they can then be zipped together in the CorpusSet class. Because in most cases we are assuming files are being brought in, we can use a StringIO object to act like a file instead, therefore mitigating the need to write temp files:

```
# test/lib/corpus_spec.rb

describe Corpus do
  let(:positive) { StringIO.new('loved movie!! loved') }
  let(:positive_corpus) { Corpus.new(positive, :positive) }

  it 'consumes a positive training set and unique set of words' do
    positive_corpus.words.must_equal Set.new(%w[loved movie])
  end
end
```

At this point, we need to implement the method #words on our Corpus. This method should return a set of words that have been passed in. This would probably look something like:

```
# lib/corpus.rb

class Corpus
  # initialize
  # tokenize
  # sentiment_code

  attr_reader :sentiment

  def words
    @words ||= begin
      set = Set.new
      @io.each_line do |line|
        Corpus.tokenize(line).each do |word|
          set << word
        end
      end
      @io.rewind
      set
    end
  end
end
```

Now that we have taken care of tokenization as well as storing all words into a unique set, we can move on to the only seam of our tool: the CorpusSet class.

The CorpusSet Class

As this point, we need to define the `CorpusSet` class. This class takes multiple `Corpus` objects and zips them together into one set of words as well as builds a vector for the `SentimentClassifier` to use. This is where the seam exists between our data and the Support Vector Machine. To reiterate, our `CorpusSet` class will be responsible for the following:

1. Zipping two `Corpus` objects
2. Building a sparse vector of both corpora

Zip two corpus objects

Our first test case will take two `Corpus` objects and combine them into one `CorpusSet` class. It will look like this:

```
# test/lib/corpus_set_spec.rb

require 'spec_helper'

describe CorpusSet do
  let(:positive) { StringIO.new('I love this country') }
  let(:negative) { StringIO.new('I hate this man') }

  let(:positive_corp) { Corpus.new(positive, :positive) }
  let(:negative_corp) { Corpus.new(negative, :negative) }

  let(:corpus_set) { CorpusSet.new([positive_corp, negative_corp]) }

  it 'composes two corpuses together' do
    corpus_set.words.must_equal %w[love country hate man]
  end
end
```

This test takes two different `Corpus` objects and mixes them together into the word set. Building this on the `CorpusSet` side, we would have something similar to this:

```
# lib/corpus_set.rb

class CorpusSet
  attr_reader :words

  def initialize(corpora)
    @corpora = corpora
    @words = corpora.reduce(Set.new) do |set, corpus|
      set.merge(corpus.words)
    end.to_a
  end
end
```

This is a simple idea; just merge the sets together into one big set. But now we need to define the seam that will tie into our `SentimentClassifier`.

Build a sparse vector that ties into SentimentClassifier

At this point, we have a set of words that are in our `CorpusSet` and we need a way of translating them to something that a Support Vector Machine can use. The most common way of doing this would be to convert incoming strings into a vector of 1s and 0s. For instance, imagine we have the corpus "The quick brown fox" and we want to determine the vector for "the fox". Our first step would be to take "the quick brown fox" and split it up into indices as shown in Table 6-1.

Table 6-1. CorpusSet words

Word	Index
the	0
quick	1
brown	2
fox	3

Now that we know what indices are attached to which words, we can take our string "the fox" and make a new row vector, which would look like Table 6-2.

Table 6-2. Row vector

Words	the	quick	brown	fox
Indices	0	1	2	3
"the fox"	1	0	0	1

So in the case of "the fox" we only set the index 0 and 3 to 1. This seems like a good idea until you realize that most times a corpus of training data can contain thousands of words and indices. So our row vectors would be over 90% 0s and under 10% 1s for each string. Instead, we should think about using a sparse vector or hash in Ruby.

Sparse Vector and Matrices

Sparse vectors are simply a compression technique for storing vectors or matrices. Say you have the vector written in Ruby:

```ruby
require 'objspace'
sparse_array = 30_000.times.map {|i| (i % 3000 == 0) ? 1 : 0}
sparse_array.size #=> 30000
ObjectSpace.memsize_of(sparse_array) #=> 302,672 bytes
```

This array has a length of 30,000! 29,990 of those are just 0s. Instead of storing all of those 0s, we can transform the array into a hash that stores only index relationships where the number is nonzero:

```ruby
sparse_hash = Hash.new(0)

sparse_array.each_with_index do |val, i|
  if val.nonzero?
    sparse_hash[i] = val
  else
    # Skip
  end
end

sparse_hash.size #=> 10
ObjectSpace.memsize_of(sparse_hash) #=> 616 bytes
```

Notice the enormous reduction in size. We went from 30,000 to 10! Sparse vectors can be generalized to be used with matrices as well:

```ruby
require 'matrix'
require 'objspace'
matrix = Matrix.build(300, 100) do |row, col|
  if  row % 3 == 0 && col % 300 == 0
    1
  else
    0
  end
end

matrix.row_size * matrix.column_size #=> 30000

# memsize_of doesn't work unless it's a C level object like an array
ObjectSpace.memsize_of(matrix.to_a.flatten) #=> 312,968 bytes

sparse_matrix = Hash.new(0)

matrix.each_with_index do |e, row, col|
  if e.nonzero?
    sparse_matrix[[row, col]] = e
  else
```

```
      # This is zero and therefore we skip it
    end
  end

  sparse_matrix.length #=> 100
  ObjectSpace.memsize_of(sparse_matrix) #=> 5,144 bytes
```

Using a sparse vector is important for memory considerations and speed; there's no need to store something that takes up more space than needed.

Using a sparse hash instead of a vector, let's build a seam test that ensures that our sentiment analyzer receives the proper information from a CorpusSet. A test would look like this:

```
# test/lib/corpus_set_spec.rb

describe CorpusSet do
  it 'returns a set of sparse vectors to train on' do
    expected_ys = [1, -1]
    expected_xes = [[0,1], [2,3]]
    expected_xes.map! do |x|
      Libsvm::Node.features(Hash[x.map {|i| [i, 1]}])
    end

    ys, xes = corpus_set.to_sparse_vectors

    ys.must_equal expected_ys

    xes.flatten.zip(expected_xes.flatten).each do |x, xp|
      x.value.must_equal xp.value
      x.index.must_equal xp.index
    end
  end
end
```

To implement this, we would write the code as follows:

```
# lib/corpus_set.rb

class CorpusSet
  # initialize

  attr_reader :words

  def to_sparse_vectors
    calculate_sparse_vectors!
    [@yes, @xes]
  end

  private
  def calculate_sparse_vectors!
    return if @state == :calculated
```

```
    @yes = []
    @xes = []
    @corpora.each do |corpus|
      vectors = load_corpus(corpus)
      @xes.concat(vectors)
      @yes.concat([corpus.sentiment_code] * vectors.length)
    end
    @state = :calculated
  end

  def load_corpus(corpus)
    vectors = []
    corpus.sentences do |sentence|
      vectors << sparse_vector(sentence)
    end
    vectors
  end
end
```

Now the `CorpusSet` can receive multiple `Corpus` objects and convert them into sparse hashes of information for the `SentimentClassifier` to use. This is where we will actually start using the SVM algorithm, and train the data.

The SentimentClassifier Class

Now that we have the portion of the app that takes training data for both positive and negative text, we can build the SVM portion of the app (the `SentimentClassifier` class). The point of this class is to take information from a `CorpusSet` and convert it into an SVM model. After it has done that, this serves as a way of taking new information and mapping it either to `:positive` or `:negative`. In addition to building the `SentimentClassifier` class, we need to address the following:

- We need something to refactor the interaction with `CorpusSet` because the API for `CorpusSet` is too complicated to use.
- We need a library to handle the SVM algorithm.
- We need something to train on and cross-validate.

Refactoring the interaction with CorpusSet

The `SentimentClassifier` takes one argument, which is a `CorpusSet`. This is simply the corpus set of all training data. Unfortunately, with our argument being a `Corpus Set`, we might run into the following syntax:

```
# lib/sentiment_classifier.rb

class SentimentClassifier
  def initialize(corpus_set)
```

```
      # Initialization
    end
  end

  positive = Corpus.new(positive_file_path, :positive)
  negative = Corpus.new(negative_file_path, :negative)
  corpus_set = CorpusSet.new([positive, negative])
  classifier = SentimentClassifier.new(corpus_set)
```

This is not good API design—it requires a lot of previous information to build a Corpus and then a CorpusSet. In reality, we want something more like a factory method that builds a SentimentClassifier. This method, .build, would take multiple arguments pointing at training data. Instead of passing in a hash, we'll just assume that positive text will have the file extension *.pos*, and negative text will have the extension *.neg*.

Making a factory method called .build will really help, and doesn't require us to explicitly build everything; it relies on the filesystem type, so we can simply fill in the blanks:

```
  # lib/sentiment_classifier.rb

  class SentimentClassifier
    def self.build(files)
      mapping = {
        '.pos' => :positive,
        '.neg' => :negative
      }

      corpora = files.map { |file| Corpus.new(file, mapping.fetch(File.extname(fil
e)) }
      corpus_set = CorpusSet.new(corpora)

      new(corpus_set)
    end
  end
```

Now that we're at this junction, we still have a couple of decision to make: what library to use to build our SVM model, and where to find training data.

Library to handle Support Vector Machines: LibSVM

When it comes to libraries to handle Support Vector Machines, most people tend to grab LibSVM. It has the longest track record, is written in C, and has many bindings, from Python to Java to Ruby. One caveat here, though, is that there are a few Ruby gems for LibSVM, and not all are superb. The gem *rb-libsvm*—which is what we will use—supports sparse vectors and therefore is best suited for our problems. There are others out there that use swig adapters and unfortunately don't support sparse matrices as well.

Training data

Up to this point, we haven't talked about training data for our tool. We need some text that is mapped as either negative or positive. These data would be organized into lines and stored in files. There are many different sources of data, but what we'll use is from GitHub (*https://github.com/jperla/sentiment-data*). This is a set of data from Pang Lee about movie review sentiment.

This is a highly specific data set and will work only for movie reviews from IMDb (the Internet Movie Database), but it is sufficient for our purposes. If you were to use this with any other program, most likely you would use a data set specific to what you were trying to solve. So, for instance, Twitter sentiment would come from actual tweets that were mapped to negative and positive. Keep in mind that it's not too difficult to build your own data set by creating a survey form and partitioning out work to Mechanical Turk by Amazon.

Cross-validating with the movie review data

Cross-validation is the best way to ensure that our data is trained well and that our model works properly. The basic idea is to take a big data set, split it into two or more pieces, and then use one of those pieces of data as training while using the other to validate against it.

In test form, it would look like this:

```ruby
# test/cross_validation_spec.rb

describe 'Cross Validation' do
  include TestMacros

  def self.test_order
    :alpha
  end

  (-15..15).each do |exponent|
    it "runs cross validation for C=#{2**exponent}" do
      neg = split_file("./config/rt-polaritydata/rt-polarity.neg")
      pos = split_file("./config/rt-polaritydata/rt-polarity.pos")

      classifier = SentimentClassifier.build([
        neg.fetch(:training),
        pos.fetch(:training)
      ])

      # find the minimum

      c = 2 ** exponent
      classifier.c = c

      n_er = validate(classifier, neg.fetch(:validation), :negative)
```

```ruby
      p_er = validate(classifier, pos.fetch(:validation), :positive)
      total = Rational(n_er.numerator + p_er.numerator, n_er.denominator + p_er.d
enominator)

      skip("Total error rate for C=#{2 ** exponent} is: #{total.to_f}")
    end
  end
end
```

We're using `skip` and `self.test_order` here. The `skip` method is used to give us information but not to test anything per se. Because we are trying to find an optimal c, we are just experimenting using tests. Also notice that we override `test_order` here and set it to `alpha`. That is because the mini-test by default uses random order, meaning that as we're going through the series from –15 to 15 we will get data out of order. It is much easier to interpret results when you're looking at them in order.

Also notice that we have introduced two new methods, `split_file` and `validate`. These are in our test macros module as:

```ruby
# test/test_macros.rb

module TestMacros
  def validate(classifier, file, sentiment)
    total = 0
    misses = 0

    File.open(file, 'rb').each_line do |line|
      if classifier.classify(line) != sentiment
        misses += 1
      else
      end
      total += 1
    end

    Rational(misses, total)
  end

  def split_file(filepath)
    ext = File.extname(filepath)
    validation = File.open("./test/fixtures/validation#{ext}", "wb")
    training = File.open("./test/fixtures/training#{ext}", "wb")

    counter = 0
    File.open(filepath, 'rb').each_line do |l|
      if (counter) % 2 == 0
        validation.write(l)
      else
        training.write(l)
      end
      counter += 1
    end
```

```
      training.close
      validation.close
    end
  end
```

In this test, we iterate from 2 through –15 all the way up to 15. This will cover most of the territory we want. After the cross-validation is done, we can pick the best C and use that for our model. Technically speaking, this is called a *grid search*, and it will attempt to find a good enough solution over a set of trial runs.

Now we need to work on the backend of the `SentimentClassifier`. This is where we use LibSVM by building our model and making a tiny state machine:

```ruby
# lib/sentiment_classifier.rb

class SentimentClassifier
  # build
  def initialize(corpus_set)
    @corpus_set = corpus_set
    @c = 2 ** 7
  end

  def c=(cc)
    @c = cc
    @model = nil
  end

  def words
    @corpus_set.words
  end

  def classify(string)
    if trained?
      prediction = @model.predict(@corpus_set.sparse_vector(string))
      present_answer(prediction)
    else
      @model = model
      classify(string)
    end
  end

  def trained?
    !!@model
  end

  def model
    puts 'starting to get sparse vectors'
    y_vec, x_mat = @corpus_set.to_sparse_vectors

    prob = Libsvm::Problem.new
    parameter = Libsvm::SvmParameter.new
    parameter.cache_size = 1000
```

```
        parameter.gamma = Rational(1, y_vec.length).to_f
        parameter.eps = 0.001

        parameter.c = @c
        parameter.kernel_type = Libsvm::KernelType::LINEAR

        prob.set_examples(y_vec, x_mat)
        Libsvm::Model.train(prob, parameter)
      end
    end
```

Here's where things get more interesting and we actually build the Support Vector Machine to work with the rest of the problem. As noted, we are using the LibSVM library, which is a standard. We first build our `sparse_vectors`, then load up a new LibSVM problem, and finally give it the default parameters.

After running the cross-validation, we see that the best C is 128, which happens to have a ~30% error rate.

Improving Results Over Time

There are a few different ways of improving the 30% error rate, which involve a bit of experimentation:

- Stripping out stop words
- Improving tokenization
- Using different polynomial kernels

You could also try out a few other algorithms with the same data to see which one works better.

Conclusion

The Support Vector Machines algorithm is very well suited for classifying two separable classes. It can be modified to separate more than two classes and doesn't suffer from the curse of dimensionality that K-Nearest Neighbors does. This chapter taught you how SVM can be used to separate loyal and disloyal customers, as well as how to assign sentiment to movie data.

## CHAPTER 7

Neural Networks

Neural Networks (or Nets) are effective at mapping observed data to a function. Researchers have been able to use Neural Networks for things like handwriting detection, computer vision, and speech recognition with breakthrough results.

Essentially, Neural Networks are an effective way of learning from data and have a long history dating back to the 1800s. In this chapter, we're going to discuss how the Neural Networks algorithm came to be, what goes into it, and how it works, as well as a practical example of classifying languages based on character frequencies.

 The Neural Networks algorithm is excellent at function approximation and supervised learning problems. It has little restrictions on what it can do and has proven quite successful in practice. However, it is limited to operating on binary inputs and can present challenges from a complexity and speed standpoint.

History of Neural Networks

When introduced, Neural Networks were about studying how the brain operates. Neurons in our brains work together in a network to process and make sense of inputs and stimuli. Alexander Bain and William James both proposed that brains operated in a network that could process lots of information. This network of neurons has the ability to recognize patterns and learn from previous data. For instance, if a child is shown a picture of eight dogs, she starts to understand what a dog looks like.

This research was expanded to include a more artificial bent when Warren McCulloch and Walter Pitts invented *threshold logic*. Threshold logic combines binary information to determine logical truth. They suggested using something called a *step function*, which attached a threshold to either accept or reject a summation of previous information.

After many years of research, Neural Networks and threshold logic were combined to form what we call an *Artificial Neural Network*.

What Is an Artificial Neural Network?

A Neural Network (see Figure 7-1) is a robust function that takes an arbitrary set of inputs and fits it to an arbitrary set of outputs that are binary. It is excellent at fuzzy matching, and building robust functions to match just about anything. In practice, Neural Networks are used in deep learning research to match images to features and much more.

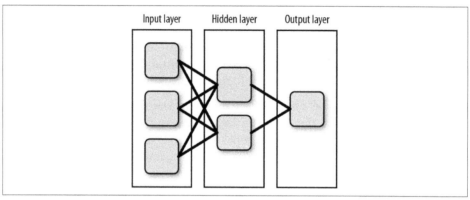

Figure 7-1. A visual representation of a Neural Network

Fuzzy matching is a general machine learning problem of trying to match inputs with outputs based on previous information.

What makes Neural Networks special is their use of a hidden layer of weighted functions called neurons, with which you can effectively build a network that maps a lot of other functions. Without a hidden layer of functions, Neural Networks would be just a set of simple weighted functions.

Neural Networks are denoted by the number of neurons per layer. For example, if we have 20 neurons in our input layer, 10 in one hidden layer, and 5 in an output layer, it would be a 20-10-5 network. If there is more than one hidden layer, then we would denote it as, say, 20-7-7-5 (the two middle 7s are layers with 7 nodes apiece).

To summarize, then, Neural Networks comprise the following parts:

- The input layer
- The hidden layer(s)
- Neurons
- The output layer
- The training algorithm

Next, I'll explain what each of these parts does and how it works.

Input Layer

The input layer, shown in Figure 7-2, is the entry point of a Neural Network. It is the entry point for the inputs you are giving to the model. There are no neurons in this layer because its main purpose is to serve as a conduit to the hidden layer(s). The input type is important, as Neural Networks work with only two types: symmetric or standard.

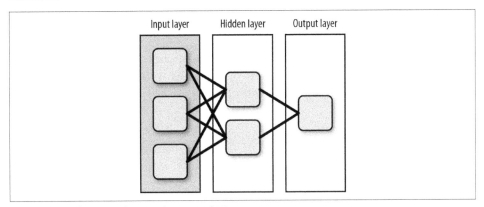

Figure 7-2. *The input layer of a Neural Net*

With training a Neural Network, we have observations and inputs. Taking the simple example of an exclusive or (also known as XOR), we have the truth table shown in Table 7-1.

Table 7-1. XOR truth table

Input A	Input B	Output
false	false	false
false	true	true
true	false	true
true	true	false

In this case, we have four observations and two inputs, which could either be true or false. Neural Networks do not work off of true or false, though, and knowing how to code the input is key. We'll need to translate these to either standard or symmetric inputs.

Standard inputs

The standard range for input values is between 0 and 1. In our previous XOR example, we would code true as 1 and false as 0.

This style of input has one downside: if your data is sparse, meaning full of 0s, it can skew results. Having a data set with lots of 0s means we risk the model breaking down. Only use standard inputs if you know that there isn't sparse data.

Symmetric inputs

Symmetric inputs avoids the issue with 0s. These are between –1 and 1. In our preceding example, –1 would be false, and 1 would be true.

This kind of input has the benefit of our model not breaking down because of the zeroing-out effect. In addition to that, it puts less emphasis on the middle of a distribution of inputs. If we introduced a "maybe" into the XOR calculation, we could map that as 0 and ignore it.

Inputs can be used in either the symmetric or standard format but need to be marked as such, as the way we calculate the output of neurons depends on this.

Hidden Layers

Without hidden layers, Neural Networks would be a set of weighted linear combinations. In other words, Neural Networks have the ability to model nonlinear data because there are hidden layers (Figure 7-3).

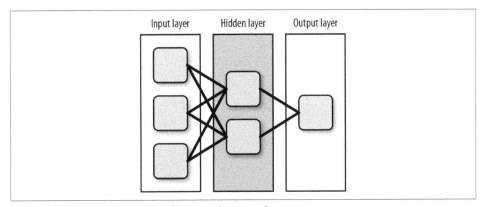

Figure 7-3. The hidden layer of a Neural Network

Each hidden layer contains a set of neurons (Figure 7-4), which then passes to the output layer.

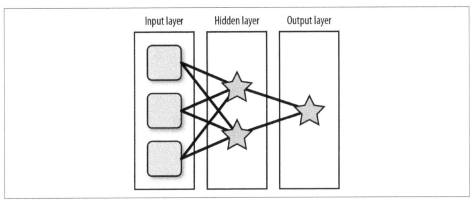

Figure 7-4. Neurons of a Neural Network

Neurons

Neurons are weighted linear combinations that are wrapped in an activation function. The weighted linear combination (or sum) is a way of aggregating all of the previous neurons' data into one output for the next layer to consume as input. Activation functions, shown in Figure 7-5, serve as a way to normalize data so it's either symmetric or standard.

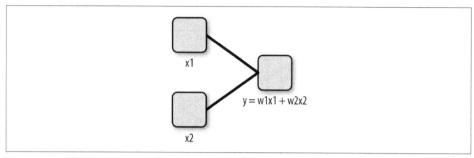

Figure 7-5. Neurons wrapped in an activation function

As a network is feeding information forward, it is aggregating previous inputs into weighted sums. We take the value *y* and compute the activated value based on an activation function.

Activation functions

As mentioned, activation functions, some of which are listed in Table 7-2, serve as a way to normalize data between either the standard or symmetric ranges. They also are differentiable, and need to be because of how we find weights in a training algorithm.

Table 7-2. Common activation functions

Name	Standard	Symmetric
Sigmoid	$\dfrac{1}{1+e^{-2sum}}$	$\dfrac{2}{1+e^{-2sum}} - 1$
Cosine	$\dfrac{\cos (sum)}{2} + 0.5$	$\cos(sum)$
Sine	$\dfrac{\sin (sum)}{2} + 0.5$	$\sin(sum)$
Gaussian	$\dfrac{1}{e^{sum^2}}$	$\dfrac{2}{e^{sum^2}} - 1$
Elliott	$\dfrac{0.5sum}{1+\mid sum \mid} + 0.5$	$\dfrac{sum}{1+\mid sum \mid}$
Linear	$sum > 1\,?\,1 : (sum < 0 : sum)$	$sum > 1\,?\,1 : (sum < -1\,?\,-1 : sum)$
Threshold	$sum < 0\,?\,0 : 1$	$sum < 0\,?\,-1 : 1$

The big advantage of using activation functions is that they serve as a way of buffering incoming values at each layer. This is useful because Neural Networks have a way of finding patterns and forgetting about the noise.

There are two main categories for activation functions: sloped or periodic. In most cases, the sloped activation functions (shown in Figures 7-6 and 7-8) are a suitable default choice. The periodic functions (shown in Figures 7-7 and 7-9) are used for modeling data with lots of noise. They generally take the form of either a sine or cosine function.

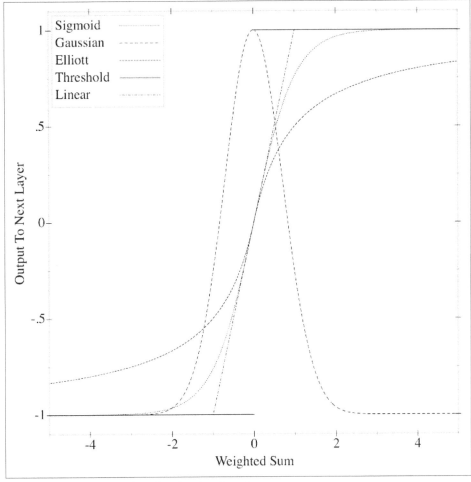

Figure 7-6. Symmetric sloped activation functions

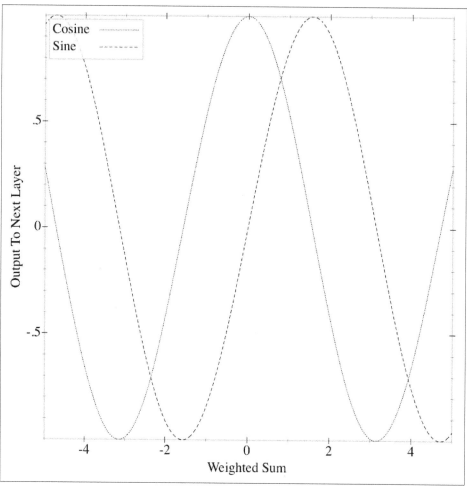

Figure 7-7. Symmetric periodic activation functions

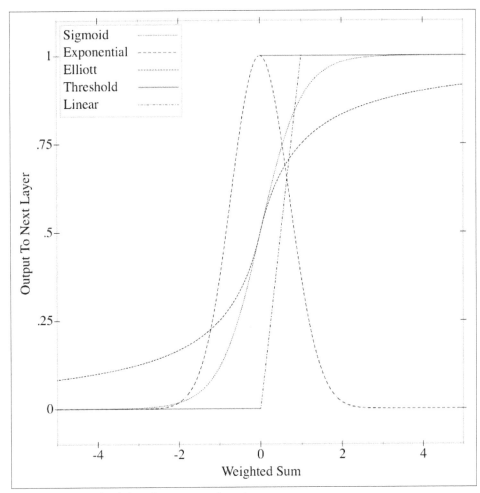

Figure 7-8. Standard sloped activation functions

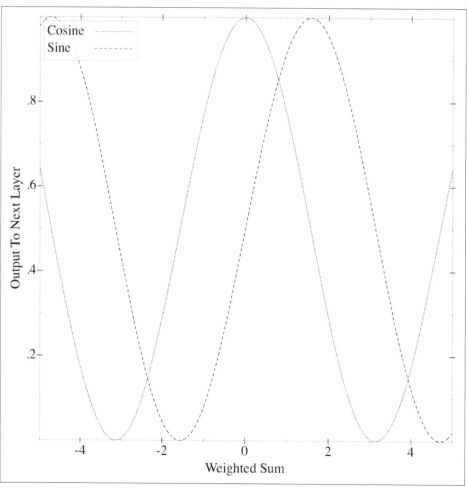

Figure 7-9. Standard periodic activation functions

Sigmoid is the default function to be used with neurons because of its ability to smooth out the decision. Elliott is a sigmoidal function that is quicker to compute, so it's the choice I make. Cosine and sine waves are used when you are mapping something that has a random-looking process associated with it. In most cases, these trigonometric functions aren't as useful to our problems.

Neurons are where all of the work is done. They are a weighted sum of previous inputs put through an activation function that either bounds it to 0 to 1 or –1 to 1. In the case of a neuron where we have two inputs before it, the function for the neuron would be $y = \phi(w_1\dot{x}_1 + w_2\dot{x}_2)$, where ϕ is an activation function like sigmoid, and w_i is weights determined by a training algorithm.

Output Layer

The output layer is similar to the input layer except that it has neurons in it. This is where the data comes out of the model. Just as with the input layer, this data will either be symmetric or standard.

Output layers decide how many neurons are output, which is a function of what we're modeling (see Figure 7-10). In the case of a function that outputs whether a stop light is red, green, or yellow, we'd have three outputs (one for each color). Each of those outputs would contain an approximation for what we want.

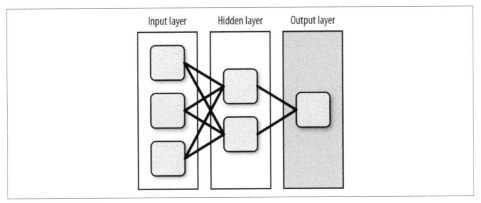

Figure 7-10. The output layer of a Neural Network

Training Algorithms

As mentioned, the weights for each neuron came from a training algorithm. There are many such algorithms, but the most common are:

- Back Propagation
- QuickProp
- RProp

All of these algorithms find optimal weights for each neuron. They do so through *iterations*, also known as *epochs*. For each epoch, a training algorithm goes through the entire Neural Network and compares it against what is expected. At this point, it learns from past miscalculations.

These algorithms have one thing in common: they are trying to find the optimal solution in a *convex error surface*. You can think of convex error surface as a bowl with a minimum value in it. Imagine that you are at the top of a hill and want to make it to a valley, but the valley is full of trees. You can't see much in front of you, but you know that you want to get to the valley. You would do so by proceeding based on local inputs and guessing where you want to go next. This is known as the Gradient

Descent algorithm (i.e., determining minimum error by walking down a valley) and it is illustrated in Figure 7-11. The training algorithms do the same thing; they are looking to minimize error by using local information.

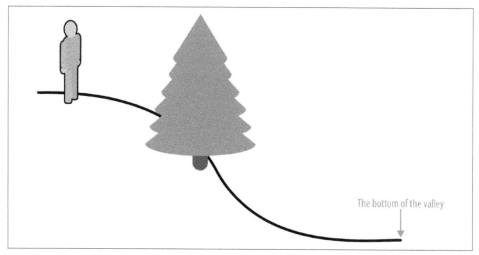

Figure 7-11. Gradient Descent algorithm in a nutshell

The delta rule

While we could solve a massive amount of equations, it would be faster to iterate. Instead of trying to calculate the derivative of the error function with respect to the weight, we calculate a change in weight for each neuron's weights. This is known as the delta rule, and it is as follows:

$$\delta w_{ji} = \alpha\left(t_j - \phi\left(h_j\right)\right)\phi'\left(h_j\right)x_i$$

This states that the change in weight for the neuron j's weight number i is:

```
alpha * (expected - calculated) * derivative_of_calculated * input_at_i
```

`alpha` is the *learning rate* and is a small constant. This initial idea, though, is what powers the idea behind the Back Propagation algorithm, or the general case of the delta rule.

Back Propagation

Back Propagation is the simplest of the three algorithms that determine the weight of a neuron. You define error as (*expected * actual*)^2 where *expected* is the expected output and *actual* is the calculated number from the neurons. We want to find where the derivative of that equals 0, which is the minimum:

$$\Delta w(t) = -\alpha(t - y)\phi' x_i + \epsilon \Delta w(t - 1)$$

ϵ is the *momentum factor* and propels previous weight changes into our current weight change, whereas α is the learning rate.

Back Propagation has the disadvantage of taking many epochs to calculate. Up until 1988, researchers were struggling to train simple Neural Networks. Their research on how to improve this led to a whole new algorithm called QuickProp.

QuickProp

Scott Fahlman introduced the QuickProp algorithm after he studied how to improve Back Propagation. He asserted that Back Propagation took too long to converge to a solution. He proposed that we instead take the biggest steps without overstepping the solution.

Fahlman determined that there are two ways to improve Back Propagation: making the momentum and learning rate dynamic, and making use of a second derivative of the error with respect to each weight. In the first case, you could better optimize for each weight, and in the second case, you could utilize Newton's method of approximating functions.

With QuickProp, the main difference from Back Propagation is that you keep a copy of the error derivative computed during the previous epoch, along with the difference between the current and previous values of this weight.

To calculate a weight change at time *t*, use the following function:

$$\Delta w(t) = \frac{S(t)}{S(t - 1) - S(t)} \dot{\Delta} w(t - 1)$$

This carries the risk of changing the weights too much, so there is a new parameter for maximum growth. No weight is allowed to be greater in magnitude than the maximum growth rate multiplied by the previous step for that weight.

RProp

RProp is the most used algorithm because it converges fast. It was introduced by Martin Riedmiller in the 1990s and has had some improvements since then. It converges on a solution quickly due to its insight that the algorithm can update the weights many times through an epoch. Instead of calculating weight changes based on a formula, it uses only the sign for change as well as an increase factor and decrease factor.

To see what this algorithm looks like in code, we need to define a few constants (or defaults). These are a way to make sure the algorithm doesn't operate forever or become volatile. These defaults were taken from the FANN library.

The basic algorithm was easier to explain in Ruby instead of writing out the partial derivatives.

 For ease of reading, note that I am not calculating the error gradients (i.e., the change in error with respect to that specific weight term).

This code gives you an idea of how the RProp algorithm works using just pure Ruby code:

```ruby
neurons = 3
inputs = 4

delta_zero = 0.1
increase_factor = 1.2
decrease_factor = 0.5
delta_max = 50.0
delta_min = 0
max_epoch = 100
deltas = Array.new(inputs) { Array.new(neurons) { delta_zero }}
last_gradient = Array.new(inputs) { Array.new(neurons) { 0.0 } }


sign = ->(x) {
  if x > 0
    1
  elsif x < 0
    -1
  else
    0
  end
}

weights = inputs.times.map {|i| rand(-1.0..1.0) }

1.upto(max_epoch) do |j|
  weights.each_with_index do |i, weight|
    # Current gradient is derived from the change of each value at each layer
    gradient_momentum = last_gradient[i][j] * current_gradient[i][j]

    if gradient_momentum > 0
      deltas[i][j] = [deltas[i][j] * increase_factor, delta_max].min
      change_weight = -sign.(current_gradient[i][j]) * deltas[i][j]
      weights[i] = weight + change_weight
      last_gradient[i][j] = current_gradient[i][j]
```

```
    elsif gradient_momentum < 0
      deltas[i][j] = [deltas[i][j] * decrease_factor, delta_min].max
      last_gradient[i][j] = 0
    else
      change_weight = -sign.(current_gradient[i][j]) * deltas[i][j]
      weights[i] = weights[i] + change_weight
      last_gradient[i][j] = current_gradient[i][j]
    end
  end
end
```

These are the fundamentals you need to understand to be able to build a Neural Network. Next, we'll talk about how to do so, and what decisions we must make to build an effective one.

Building Neural Networks

Before you begin building a Neural Network, you must answer the following questions:

- How many hidden layers should you use?
- How many neurons per layer?
- What is your tolerance for error?

How Many Hidden Layers?

As noted earlier in this chapter, what makes Neural Networks unique is their usage of hidden layers. If you took out hidden layers, you'd have a linear combination problem. You aren't bound to use any number of hidden layers, but there are three heuristics that help:

- *Do not use more than two hidden layers; otherwise, you might overfit the data.* With too many layers, the network starts to memorize the training data. Instead, we want it to find patterns.
- *One hidden layer will do the job of approximating a continuous mapping.* This is the common case. Most neural networks have only one hidden layer in them.
- *Two hidden layers will be able to push past a continuous mapping.* This is an uncommon case, but if you know that you don't have a continuous mapping, you can use two hidden layers.

There is no steadfast rule holding you to these heuristics for picking the number of hidden layers. It comes down to trying to minimize the risk of overfitting or underfitting your data.

How Many Neurons for Each Layer?

Neural Networks are excellent aggregators and terrible expanders. Neurons themselves are weighted sums of previous neurons, so they have a tendency to not expand out as well as they combine. If you think about it, a hidden layer of 2 that goes to an output layer of 30 would mean that for each output neuron, there would be two inputs. There just isn't enough entropy or data to make a well-fitted model.

This idea of emphasizing aggregation over expansion leads us to the next set of heuristics:

- The number of hidden neurons should be between the number of inputs and the number of neurons at the output layer.
- The number of hidden neurons should be two-thirds the size of the input layer, plus the size of the output layer.
- The number of hidden neurons should be less than twice the size of the input layer.

This comes down to trial and error, though, as the number of hidden neurons will influence how well the model cross-validates, as well as the convergence on a solution. This is just a starting point.

Tolerance for Error and Max Epochs

The tolerance for error gives us a time to stop training. We will never get to a perfect solution but rather converge on one. If you want an algorithm that performs well, then the error rate might be low, like 0.01%. But in most cases, that will take a long time to train due to its intolerance for error.

Many start with an error tolerance of 1%. Through cross-validation, this might need to be tightened even more. In Neural Network parlance, the tolerance is internal, is measured as a mean squared error, and defines a stopping place for the network.

Neural Networks are trained over epochs, and this is set before the training algorithm even starts. If an algorithm is taking 10,000 iterations to get to a solution, then there might be a high risk for overtraining and creating a sensitive network. A starting point for training is 1,000 epochs or iterations to train over. This way, you can model some complexity without getting too carried away.

Both max epochs and maximum error define our converging points. They serve as a way to signal when the training algorithm can stop and yield the Neural Network. At this point, we've learned enough to get our hands dirty and try a real-world example.

Using a Neural Network to Classify a Language

Characters used in a language have a direct correlation with the language itself. Mandarin is recognizable due to its characters, because each character means a specific word. The same is true with many Latin-based languages, but in regards to letter frequency.

If we look at the difference of "The quick brown fox jumped over the lazy dog" in English and its German equivalent, "Der schnelle braune Fuchs sprang über den faulen Hund", we'd get the frequency chart shown in Table 7-3.

Table 7-3. Difference in frequency between English and German sentence

	a	b	c	d	e	f	g	h	i	j	k	l	m	n	o	p	q	r	s	t	u	v	w	x	y	z	ü
English	1	1	1	2	4	1	1	2	1	1	1	1	1	1	4	1	1	2	0	2	2	1	1	1	1	1	0
German	3	2	2	3	7	2	1	3	0	0	0	3	0	6	0	1	0	4	2	0	4	0	0	0	0	1	1
Difference	2	1	1	1	3	1	0	1	1	1	1	2	1	5	4	0	1	2	2	2	2	1	1	1	1	0	1

There is a subtle difference between German and English. German uses quite a few more Ns, whereas English uses a lot of Os. If we wanted to expand this to a few more European languages, how would we do that? More specifically, how can we build a model to classify sentences written in English, Polish, German, Finnish, Swedish, or Norwegian?

In this case, we'll build a simple model to predict a language based on the frequency of the characters in the sentences. But before we start, we need to have some data. For that, we'll use the most translated book in the world: the Bible. Let's extract all the chapters out of Matthew and Acts.

The approach we will take is to extract all the sentences out of these text files and create vectors of frequency normalized between 0 and 1. From that, we will train a network that will take those inputs and then match them to a vector of 6. The vector of 6 is defined as the index of the language equaling 1. If the language we are using to train is index 3, the vector would look like [0,0,0,1,0,0] (zero-based indexing).

Setup Notes

All of the code we're using for this example can be found on Git-Hub (*http://bit.ly/1x21Pi3*).

Ruby is constantly changing, so the *README* file is the best place to get up to speed on running the examples.

Grabbing the Data

If you want to grab the data, I wrote the following script to help you download it from *Biblegateway.com*:

```ruby
require 'nokogiri'
require 'open-uri'

url = "http://www.biblegateway.com/passage/"

languages = {
  'English' => {
    'version' => 'ESV',
    'search' => ['Matthew', 'Acts']
  },
  'Polish' => {
    'version' => 'SZ-PL',
    'search' => ['Ewangelia+według+św.+Mateusza', 'Dzieje+Apostolskie']
  },
  'German' => {
    'version' => 'HOF',
    'search' => ['Matthaeus', 'Apostelgeschichte']
  },
  'Finnish' => {
    'version' => 'R1933',
    'search' => ['Matteuksen', 'Teot']
  },
  'Swedish' => {
    'version' => 'SVL',
    'search' => ['Matteus', 'Apostlagärningarna']
  },
  'Norwegian' => {
    'version' => 'DNB1930',
    'search' => ['Matteus', 'Apostlenes-gjerninge']
  }
}

languages.each do |language, search_pattern|
  text = ''

  search_pattern['search'].each_with_index do |search, i|
    1.upto(28).each do |page|
      puts "Querying #{language} #{search} chapter #{page}"
```

```
          uri = [
            url,
            URI.encode_www_form({
              search: "#{URI.escape(search)}+#{page}",
              version: "#{search_pattern.fetch('version')}"
            })
          ].join('?')
          puts uri
          doc = Nokogiri::HTML.parse(open(uri))
          doc.css('.passage p').each do |verse|
            text += verse.inner_text.downcase.gsub(/[\d,;:\\\-\"]/,'')
          end
        end
        File.open("#{language}_#{i}.txt", 'wb') {|f| f.write(text)}
      end
    end
```

This will download and store Acts and Matthew verses in multiple languages. Feel free to try more languages!

Writing the Seam Test for Language

To take our training data, we need to build a class to parse that and interface with our Neural Network. For that, we will use the class name Language. The Language's purpose is to take a file of text in a given language and load it into a distribution of character frequencies. When needed, the Language will output a vector of these characters, all summing up to 1. All of our inputs will be between 0 and 1. Our parameters are:

- We want to make sure that our data is correct and sums to 1.

- We don't want characters like UTF-8 spaces or punctuation entering our data.

- We want to downcase all characters. *A* should be translated as *a*. *Ä* should also be *ä*.

This helps us to make sure that our Language class, which takes a text file and outputs an array of hashes, is correct:

```
# encoding: utf-8
# test/lib/language_spec.rb

require 'spec_helper'
require 'stringio'


describe Language do
  let(:language_data) {
    <<-EOL
    abcdefghijklmnopqrstuvwxyz.
```

```
    ABCDEFGHIJKLMNOPQRSTUVWXYZ.
    \u00A0.
    !~@#$\%^&*()_\+'?[]""''‛—<>»«›‹-„/.
    ïëéüòèöäÖßÜøæååØóąłżźśęńśćźł.
    EOL
  }

  let(:special_characters) { language_data.split("\n").last.strip }

  let(:language_io) { StringIO.new(language_data) }

  let(:language) { Language.new(language_io, 'English') }

  it 'has the proper keys for each vector' do
    language.vectors.first.keys.must_equal ('a'..'z').to_a
    language.vectors[1].keys.must_equal ('a'..'z').to_a

    special_chars = "ïëéüòèöäÖßÜøæååØóąłżźśęńśćź".split(//).uniq.sort

    language.vectors.last.keys.sort.must_equal special_chars
  end

  it 'sums to 1 for all vectors' do
    language.vectors.each do |vector|
      vector.values.inject(&:+).must_equal 1
    end
  end

  it 'returns characters that is a unique set of characters used' do
    chars = ('a'..'z').to_a
    chars.concat "ïëéüòèöäÖßÜøæååØóąłżźśęńśćź".split(//).uniq

    language.characters.to_a.sort.must_equal chars.sort
  end
end
```

At this point, we have not written Language, and all of our tests fail. For the first goal, let's get something that counts all the alpha characters and stops on a sentence. That would look like this:

```
# encoding: utf-8

# lib/language.rb

class Language
  attr_reader :name, :characters, :vectors
  def initialize(language_io, name)
    @name = name
    @vectors, @characters = Tokenizer.tokenize(language_io)
  end
end
```

```ruby
# lib/tokenizer.rb

module Tokenizer
  extend self
  PUNCTUATION = %w[~ @ # $ % ^ & * ( ) _ + ' [ ] " " ' ' - < > » « › ‹ - „ /]
  SPACES = [" ", "\u00A0", "\n"]
  STOP_CHARACTERS = ['.', '?', '!']

  def tokenize(blob)
    unless blob.respond_to?(:each_char)
      raise 'Must implement each_char on blob'
    end

    vectors = []
    dist = Hash.new(0)

    characters = Set.new
    blob.each_char do |char|
      if STOP_CHARACTERS.include?(char)
        vectors << normalize(dist) unless dist.empty?
        dist = Hash.new(0)
      elsif SPACES.include?(char) || PUNCTUATION.include?(char)

      else
        character = char.downcase.tr("ÄÀÜÖËÏŚŻŁ", "äàüöëïśżł")
        characters << character
        dist[character] += 1
      end
    end
    vectors << normalize(dist) unless dist.empty?

    [vectors, characters]
  end
end
```

Now we have something that should work. There are a couple of interesting things to note. First, special characters like *Ä* do not get downcased to *ä*. For that, you have to use `String#tr`. Second, there is a Unicode space, which is denoted as `\u00a0`.

Now we have a new problem, though, which is that the data does not add up to 1. We will introduce a new function `normalize`, which takes a hash of values and applies the function *x/sum(x)* to all values. Note that I use `Rational`, which is a 1.9.x feature that increases the reliability of calculations and doesn't do floating-point arithmetic until needed:

```ruby
# lib/tokenizer.rb

module Tokenizer
  # tokenize

  def normalize(hash)
    sum = hash.values.inject(&:+)
```

```
    Hash[
      hash.map do |k,v|
        [k, Rational(v,  sum)]
      end
    ]
  end
end
```

Everything is green and things look great for Language. We have full test coverage on a class that will be used to interface with our Neural Network. Now we can move on to building a Network class.

Cross-Validating Our Way to a Network Class

I used the Bible to find training data for our language classification because it is the most translated book in history. For the data, I decided to download Matthew and Acts in English, Finnish, German, Norwegian, Polish, and Swedish. With this natural divide between Acts and Matthew, we can define 12 tests of a model trained with Acts and see how it compares to Matthew's data, and vice versa.

The code looks like:

```
# test/cross_validation_spec.rb
# encoding: utf-8

require 'spec_helper'

# This is important because training neural networks every time a test is run
# can be a bit slow. This hash caches the networks.

networks = {}

describe Network do
  def language_name(text_file)
    File.basename(text_file, '.txt').split('_').first
  end

  def compare(network, text_file)
    misses = 0.0
    hits = 0.0

    file = File.read(text_file)

    file.split(/[\.!\?]/).each do |sentence|
      sentence_name = network.run(sentence).name

      if sentence_name == language_name(text_file)
        hits += 1
      else
        misses += 1
      end
```

```
    end

    total = misses + hits

    assert(
      misses < (0.05 * total),
      "#{text_file} has failed with a miss rate of #{misses / total}"
    )
  end

  def load_glob(glob)
    Dir[File.expand_path(glob, __FILE__)].map do |m|
      Language.new(File.open(m, 'r+'), language_name(m))
    end
  end

  let(:matthew_languages) { load_glob('../../data/*_0.txt') }
  let(:acts_languages) { load_glob('../../data/*_1.txt') }

  let(:matthew_verses) {
    networks[:matthew] ||= Network.new(matthew_languages).train!
    networks[:matthew]
  }

  let(:acts_verses) {
    networks[:acts] ||= Network.new(acts_languages).train!
    networks[:acts]
  }

  %w[English Finnish German Norwegian Polish Swedish].each do |lang|
    it "Trains and cross-validates with an error of 5% for #{lang}" do
      compare(matthew_verses, "./data/#{lang}_1.txt")
      compare(acts_verses, "./data/#{lang}_0.txt")
    end
  end
end
```

There is a folder called *data* in the root of the project that contains files in the form *Language_0.txt* and *Language_1.txt* where *Language* is the language name, _0 is the index mapping to Matthew, and _1 is the index mapping to Acts.

It takes a while to train a neural network, so I'm training only two networks, one for Acts chapters and one for Matthew chapters. At this point, we have 12 tests defined. Of course, nothing will work now because we haven't written the Network class. To start out the Network class we define an initial class as taking an array of Language classes. Secondly, because we don't want to write all the Neural Network by hand, we're using a library called Ruby-Fann, which interfaces with FANN. Our main goal initially is to get a Neural Network to accept and train.

Filling in the pieces from the previous test, we would build our network object as such:

```ruby
# lib/network.rb

require 'ruby-fann'

class Network
  def initialize(languages, error = 0.005)
    @languages = languages
    @inputs = @languages.map {|l| l.characters.to_a }.flatten.uniq.sort
    @fann = :not_ran
    @trainer = :not_trained
    @error = error
  end

  def train!
    build_trainer!
    build_standard_fann!
    @fann.train_on_data(@trainer, 1000, 10, @error)
    self
  end

  def code(vector)
    return [] if vector.nil?
    @inputs.map do |i|
      vector.fetch(i, 0.0)
    end
  end

  private
  def build_trainer!
    payload = {
      :inputs => [],
      :desired_outputs => []
    }

    @languages.each_with_index do |language, index|
      inputs = []
      desired_outputs = [0] * @languages.length
      desired_outputs[index] = 1

      language.vectors.each do |vector|
        inputs << code(vector)
      end

      payload[:inputs].concat(inputs)

      language.vectors.length.times do
        payload[:desired_outputs] << desired_outputs
      end
    end
```

```
    @trainer = RubyFann::TrainData.new(payload)
  end

  def build_standard_fann!
    hidden_neurons = (2 * (@inputs.length + @languages.length)) / 3

    @fann = RubyFann::Standard.new(
      :num_inputs => @inputs.length,
      :hidden_neurons => [ hidden_neurons ],
      :num_outputs => @languages.length
    )

    # Note that the library misspells Elliott
    @fann.set_activation_function_hidden(:elliot)
  end
end
```

Now that we have the proper inputs and the proper outputs, the model is set up and we should be able to run the whole *cross_validation_test.rb*. But, of course, there is an error because we cannot run new data against the network. To address this, we need to build a function called #run. At this point, we have something that works and looks like this:

```
# lib/network.rb

require 'ruby-fann'
class Network
  # initialize
  # train!
  # code

  def run(sentence)
    if @trainer == :not_trained || @fann == :not_ran
      raise 'Must train first call method train!'
    else
      vectors, characters = Tokenizer.tokenize(sentence)
      output_vector = @fann.run(code(vectors.first))
      @languages[output_vector.index(output_vector.max)]
    end
  end
end
```

This is where things get interesting, as it appears that German, English, Swedish, and Norwegian are all failing our test. Because our code works, now we are at the stage where we tune our Neural Network based on unit tests.

We have set our standards high, but we can reach them by tuning the network.

Tuning the Neural Network

At this point, we change the activation function to the Elliott function, which improves the results by only failing Norwegian, Swedish, and German. English dropped out of the errors, but our epochs went up just a bit. Halving the internal error rate to 0.005 is our next step, which we do by changing the last argument for @fann.train_on_data to 0.005. Finally things work and we've achieved our goal.

I'll leave further tuning to you as an exercise in playing around with what works and what does not. You can try many different activation functions, as well as internal rates of decay or errors. The takeaway here is that with an initial test to base accuracy against, you can try many different avenues.

Convergence Testing

Before continuing, you can reset the max epochs in the network class to have 20–50% over what you saw, just to make sure that over time things don't start taking forever. In our case, I saw around 200 epochs for the model to train, so I'll reset the max epochs to 300.

Precision and Recall for Neural Networks

Going a step further, when we deploy this Neural Network code to a production environment, we need to close the information loop by introducing a precision and recall metric to track over time. This metric will be calculated from user input.

We can measure precision and recall by asking in our user interface whether our prediction was correct. From this text, we can capture the blurb and the correct classification, and feed that back into our model the next time we train.

To learn more about monitoring precision and recall, see Chapter 9.

What we need to monitor the performance of this Neural Network in production is a metric for how many times a classification was run, as well as how many times it was wrong.

Wrap-Up of Example

The Neural Networks algorithm is a fun way of mapping information and learning through iterations, and it works well for our case of mapping sentences to languages. Loading this code in an IRB session, I had fun trying out phrases like "meep moop," which is classified as Norwegian! Feel free to play with the code.

Conclusion

The Neural Networks algorithm is a powerful tool in a machine learning toolkit. Neural Networks serve as a way of mapping previous observations through a functional model. While they are touted as black box models, they can be understood with a little bit of mathematics and illustration. You can use Neural Networks for many things, like mapping letter frequencies to languages or handwriting detection. There are many problems being worked on right now with regards to this algorithm, and more in-depth books on the topic as well. Anything written by Geoffrey Hinton is worth a read, namely *Unsupervised Learning: Foundations of Neural Computation* (Computational Neuroscience).

This chapter introduced Neural Networks as an artificial version of our brain and explained how they work by summing up inputs using a weighted function. These weighted functions were then normalized within a certain range. Many algorithms exist to train these weight values, but the most prevalent is the RProp algorithm. Then we summed it all up with a practical example on mapping sentences to languages.

## CHAPTER 8

Clustering

If you've been to a library, you've seen clustering at work. The Dewey Decimal System is a form of clustering. Dewey came up with a system that would attach a number of increasing granularity and in doing so, revolutionized libraries.

This idea of categorizing data points, or books, into groups is useful for organizing information. We don't know what specific category they should belong to, so we just want to split the books into a set of categories.

This type of problem is much different than what we've encountered before. All of the problems we have looked at thus far have attempted to figure out the best functional approximation to assign to a given data set and its labels. Now we are more concerned with the data itself, not the labels.

As you will see in this chapter, clustering has one downside, which is that it doesn't lend itself to use as well as other algorithms. This is called the *impossibility theorem*.

In this chapter, we will talk about clustering in general as it applies to cohorts of users, and then introduce *K*-Means clustering and Expectation Maximization (EM) clustering. Finally, we'll finish with an example about clustering jazz records into groups based on styles.

 The Clustering algorithm is an unsupervised learning problem and is great for grouping data. It can present issues, though, with application to problems; that is, it suffers from the impossibility theorem.

User Cohorts

Grouping people into cohorts (clusters) makes a lot of business and marketing sense. For instance, your first customer is different from your ten thousandth customer or millionth customer. This process of defining users into cohorts is a common one. If we are to effectively split our customers into different buckets based on behavior and time of signup, then we can better serve them by diversifying our marketing strategy.

The problem is that we don't have a predefined label for customer cohorts. To solve this problem, you could look at what month and year each person became a customer. But that is making a big assumption about the time of first purchase being the defining factor that splits customers into groups. What if the time of first purchase had nothing to do with whether customers were in one cohort or the other? For example, they could have made only that one purchase or they may have made many since then.

Instead, we should group users into cohorts based on what we *do* know about our users. For instance, let's say we know when they signed up, the amount they've spent, and what their favorite color is. Over the last two years, we've had only 10 users sign up (I hope you'd have more than that over two years, but let's keep this simple). Table 8-1 shows the data we've collected about them over that time.

Table 8-1. Data collected over two years

User ID	Signup date	Money spent	Favorite color
1	Jan 14	$40	N/A
2	Nov 3	$50	Orange
3	Jan 30	$53	Green
4	Oct 3	$100	Magenta
5	Feb 1	$0	Cyan
6	Dec 31	$0	Purple
7	Sep 3	$0	Mauve
8	Dec 31	$0	Yellow
9	Jan 13	$14	Blue
10	Jan 1	$50	Beige

Given this data, we want to define a mapping from each user to a cohort. Looking at these rows, you notice that the favorite colors are irrelevant data. This information does not provide a meaningful way of grouping our users into a cohort. That leaves us with *Money spent* and *Signup date*. There seems to be a group of users who spend money, and those who don't. In the *Signup date* column, you'll notice that there are a lot of users who sign up around the very beginning and end of the year as well as around September, October, or November.

We now need to decide on the number of clusters we want to make. Because our data set is so small, we'll just split it into two pieces. That means that we can split the cohorts into something like Table 8-2.

Table 8-2. Manual cohort assignment to the original data set

User Id	Signup date (days to Jan 1)	Money spent	Cohort
1	Jan 14 (13)	$40	1
2	Nov 3 (59)	$50	2
3	Jan 30 (29)	$53	1
4	Oct 3 (90)	$100	2
5	Feb 1 (31)	$0	1
6	Dec 31 (1)	$0	1
7	Sep 3 (120)	$0	2
8	Dec 31 (1)	$0	1
9	Jan 13 (12)	$14	1
10	Jan 1 (0)	$50	1

We have divided the customers into two groups: group 1 contains seven customers, which we could call the "beginning of the year" signups, and group 2 contains the other three.

What if we were to do this more algorithmically, though? In the next sections, we'll touch on what *K*-Means clustering is, as well as introduce EM clustering in the theoretical sense. Then we'll wrap up this chapter with an example of how to categorize a record collection on a bookshelf.

K-Means Clustering

There are a lot of clustering algorithms, like Linkage clustering or DIANA, but one of the most common is *K*-Means clustering. Using a predefined *K*, which is the number of clusters we want to split the data into, *K*-Means will find the most optimal centroid of clusters. The nicest properties of *K*-Means clustering are that the clusters will be strict and spherical in nature, and it converges to a solution.

Next, we will briefly talk about how *K*-Means Clustering works.

The K-Means Algorithm

The *K*-Means algorithm starts with a base case. Pick *K* random points in the data set and define them to be centroids. Then, for each point, assign it to a cluster number that is closest to each different centroid. Now we have a clustering based on the original randomized centroid. But that is not exactly what we want to end with, so we update where the centroids are using a mean of the data. Then, we repeat until the centroids no longer move (see Figure 8-1).

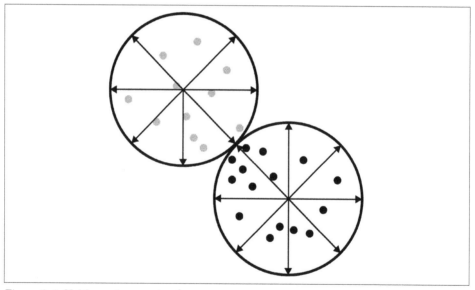

Figure 8-1. K-Means is very circular

Some possible ways of calculating the distance in *K*-Means (which we talked about in Chapter 3) are:

Manhattan distance

$$d_{manhattan}(x, y) = \Sigma_{i=1}^{n} |x_i - y_i|$$

Euclidean distance

$$d_{euclid}(x, y) = \sqrt{\Sigma_{i=1}^{n}(x_i - y_i)^2}$$

Minkowski distance

$$d(x, y) = \left(\Sigma_{i=1}^{n}|x_i - y_i|^p\right)^{\frac{1}{p}}$$

Mahalanobis distance

$$d(x, y) = \sqrt{\Sigma_{i=1}^{n}\frac{(x_i - y_i)^2}{s_i^2}}$$

The Downside of K-Means Clustering

The downside of *K*-Means clustering is that everything must have a hard boundary. This means that a data point can be in only one cluster; it can't straddle the line between the two. On top of that, *K*-Means prefers spherical data, as most of the time the Euclidean distance is being used. The downsides are obvious when you look at a graphic like Figure 8-1 where the data in the middle could really go either direction, to cluster 1 or 2.

Expectation Maximization (EM) Clustering

Instead of focusing on finding a centroid and then data points that relate to it, Expectation Maximization (EM) clustering focuses on solving a different problem. Let's say that you want to split your data points into two sections, either cluster 1 or 2. You want a good guess as to whether the data is in either cluster, but don't care if there's some fuzziness. Instead of getting an assignment, we really want a probability that the data point is in each cluster.

Unlike K-Means clustering, which focuses on making definite boundaries between clusters, EM clustering is robust to data points that might be in either cluster. This can be quite useful for classifying data that doesn't have a definite boundary.

To start with EM clustering, we make a vector called z_k = <0.5, 0.5>, which holds the probability of whether the row vector k is in either cluster. Through iterations, we find out something more like z_k = <0.9, 0.1>. Imagine you have a set of data points and instead of circling different clusters like before we assign a shade to each one.

The darker it is, the more Cluster 2 it becomes, while the lighter grays become Cluster 1, as shown in Figure 8-2.

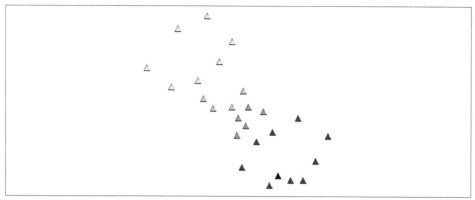

Figure 8-2. EM clustering shows how clusters can actually be much softer

The EM algorithm is split into two pieces, the expectation step and the maximization step.

The expectation step is where the probabilities get calculated given how the data currently looks and the value of our initial z_k. We calculate the log likelihood function with respect to the conditional distribution of Z given X under the current estimate of the parameters of Theta (t):

$$Q(\theta \| \theta_t) = E_{Z \| X, \theta_t}[logL(\theta; X, Z)]$$

Next, the maximization step is finding the parameter θ that maximizes the probability of θ given θ_t:

$$\theta_t = \text{arg } \max_\theta Q(\theta \| \theta_t)$$

The disadvantage of EM clustering is that it does not converge necessarily and can falter when you're mapping data with singular covariances. We will delve into more of the issues related to EM clustering in the example section. First, though, we need to talk about one feature that all clustering algorithms have in common: the *impossibility theorem*.

The Impossibility Theorem

There is no such thing as a free lunch, and clustering is no exception. The benefit we get out of clustering to magically map data points to particular groupings comes at a cost, as was laid out by Jon Kleinberg, who coined the impossibility theorem.

The theorem states that you can never have more than two of the following attributes:

- Richness
- Scale invariance
- Consistency

Richness is the notion that there exists a distance function that will yield all different types of partitions. What this means intuitively is that a clustering algorithm has the ability to create all types of mappings from data points to cluster assignments.

Scale invariance is simple to understand. Imagine that you were building a rocketship and started calculating everything in kilometers until your boss said that you need to use miles instead. There wouldn't be a problem switching; you just need to divide by a constant on all your measurements. It is scale invariant. Basically, if the numbers are all multiplied by 20, then the same cluster should happen.

Consistency is more subtle. Similar to scale invariance, if we shrank the distance between points inside a cluster and expanded them, the cluster should yield the same result. At this point, you probably understand that clustering isn't as good as you might have thought initially. It has a lot of issues, and consistency is definitely one that should be called out.

For our purposes, *K*-Means and EM clustering satisfy richness and scale invariance, but not consistency. This fact makes testing clustering just about impossible. The only way we really can test is by anecdote and example. But that is OK for analysis purposes.

In the next section, we will analyze jazz music using *K*-Means and EM clustering.

Categorizing Music

Music has a deep history of recordings as well as composed pieces. You could have an entire degree and study musicology just to be able to effectively categorize these sheets of music.

The ways we can split music into categories are endless. Personally, I split my own record collection by artist name. But artists will often collaborate. Other people prefer to categorize based on genre. But what about the fact that genres are broad? Take jazz, for instance; according to the Montreux Jazz Festival (*http://bit.ly/1DbpsGj*), jazz is anything you can improv over.

How can we effectively build a library of music where we can split up our collection into similar pieces of work?

Setup Notes

All of the code we're using for this example can be found on GitHub (*http://bit.ly/Zn3ikM*).

In this section, we will first determine where we will get our data from, what sort of attributes we can extract on, and what we can validate based on. We will also discuss why clustering sounds great in theory but in practice doesn't give us much—except for clusters, that is.

Ruby is constantly changing, so the *README* file is the best place to get up to speed on running the examples.

Let's approach this by using *K*-Means and EM clustering. By the end, we will have a soft clustering of music pieces that we can utilize to build a taxonomy of music.

We will not be using a test-driven approach to writing a clusterer, because clustering is a problem that doesn't lend itself well to hypothesis testing. This is a very important point. On the surface, clustering seems like a great solution to all problems, but in reality, it doesn't work well for actually testing our assumptions.

Remember from our earlier discussion of the impossibility theorem that we can't have a clustering algorithm that is consistent, rich, *and* scale invariant (it can only ever be two of these at most). In many ways, clustering is a data analysis tool, but it's not something we should use to solve problems that we want to control.

Gathering the Data

There is a massive amount of music data from the 1100s through today. We have MP3s, CDs, vinyl records, and written music. Without trying to classify the entire world of music, let's determine a small subsection that we can use. I don't want to be involved in any copyright suits, so we will only use public information on albums. This would be artist, song name, genre (if available), as well as characteristics that we can find on the music. To achieve this, we will access the plethora of information contained on *Discogs.com*, which contains lots of XML data dumps of records and songs.

Also, because we aren't trying to cluster the entire data set of albums in existence, let's just focus on jazz. Most people would agree that jazz is a genre that is hard to really classify into any category. It could be fusion, it could be steel drums, and so on.

So to get our data set, I downloaded the best jazz albums according to the website (*http://www.scaruffi.com/jazz/best100.html*).

The data goes back to 1940 and well into the 2000s. In total, I was able to download about 1,200 unique records. All great albums!

But that isn't enough information. On top of that, I annotated the information by using the Discogs API to determine the style of jazz in each.

After annotating the original data set, I found that there are 128 unique styles associated with jazz (at least according to Discogs). They range from aboriginal to vocal.

Analyzing the Data with K-Means

Like we did with the *K*-Nearest Neighbors algorithm, we need to figure out an optimal *K*. Unfortunately, with clustering there really isn't much we can test except to simply see whether we can split the data into two different clusters.

But let's say that we want to fit all of our records on a bookshelf and we have 25 slots. We could run a clustering of all of our data using $K = 25$.

Doing so requires little code because we have the ai4r gem to rely on:

```ruby
# lib/kmeans_clusterer.rb

require 'csv'
require 'ai4r'

data = []

artists = []
CSV.foreach('./annotated_jazz_albums.csv', :headers => true) do |row|
  @headers ||= row.headers[2..-1]
  artists << row['artist_album']
  data << row.to_h.values[2..-1].map(&:to_i)
end

ds = Ai4r::Data::DataSet.new(:data_items => data, :data_labels => @headers)
clusterer = Ai4r::Clusterers::KMeans.new
clusterer.build(ds, 25)

CSV.open('./clustered_kmeans.csv', 'wb') do |csv|
  csv << %w[artist_album year cluster]
  ds.data_items.each_with_index do |dd, i|
    csv << [artists[i], dd.first, clusterer.eval(dd)]
  end
end
```

That's it! Of course, clustering without looking at what it actually tells us is useless. This code does split the data into 25 different categories, but what does it all mean?

Looking at the graphic in Figure 8-3, which compares year versus assigned cluster number yields interesting results.

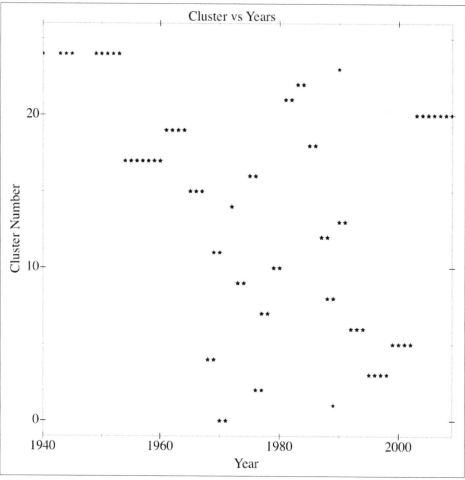

Figure 8-3. K-Means applied to jazz albums

As you can see, jazz starts out in the big band era, pretty much in the same cluster, after which it transitions into cool jazz. Then, around 1959, it starts to go in all different directions until about 1990 when things cool down a bit.

What's fascinating is how well the clustering syncs up with jazz history.

What happens when we cluster the data using EM clustering instead?

EM Clustering

With EM clustering, remember that we are probabilistically assigning to different clusters: it isn't 100% one or the other. This could be highly useful for our purposes here, as jazz has so much crossover.

There are no Ruby gems that have EM clustering in them, so we'll have to write our own version of the tool.

Let's go through the process of building our own gem and then utilize it to map the same data that we have from our jazz data set.

Our first step is to initialize the cluster. Remember, we need to have indicator variables z_i, which follows a uniform distribution. These tell us the probability that each data point is in each cluster. To do this, we have:

```
# lib/em_clusterer.rb

require 'matrix'

class EMClusterer
  attr_reader :partitions, :data, :labels, :classes

  def initialize(k, data)
    @k = k
    @data = data
    setup_cluster!
  end

  def setup_cluster!
    @labels = Array.new(@data.row_size) { Array.new(@k) { 1.0 / @k }}

    @width = @data.column_size
    @s = 0.2

    pick_k_random_indices = @data.row_size.times.to_a.shuffle.sample(@k)

    @classes = @k.times.map do |cc|
      {
        :means => @data.row(pick_k_random_indices.shift),
        :covariance => @s * Matrix.identity(@width)
      }
    end
    @partitions = []
  end
end
```

At this point, we have set up all of our base case code. We have @k, which is the number of clusters; @data, the data we pass in that we want to cluster; @labels, an array of the probability that the row is in each cluster; @classes, which holds on to an array of means and covariances that tells us where the distribution of data is. And finally, there's *@partitions*, which is the assignments of each data row to cluster index.

Now we need to build our expectation step, which is to figure out the probability of each data row in each cluster. To do this, we need to write a new method, expect:

```ruby
# lib/em_clusterer.rb

class EMClusterer
  # initialize
  # setup_cluster!

  def expect
    @classes.each_with_index do |klass, i|
      puts "Expectation for class #{i}"

      inv_cov = if klass[:covariance].regular?
        klass[:covariance].inv
      else
        puts "Applying shrinkage"
        (klass[:covariance] - (0.0001 * Matrix.identity(@width))).inv
      end

      d = Math::sqrt(klass[:covariance].det)

      @data.row_vectors.each_with_index do |row, j|
        rel = row - klass[:means]

        p = d * Math::exp(-0.5 * fast_product(rel, inv_cov))
        @labels[j][i] = p
      end
    end

    @labels = @labels.map.each_with_index do |probabilities, i|
      sum = probabilities.inject(&:+)

      @partitions[i] = probabilities.index(probabilities.max)

      if sum.zero?
        probabilities.map { 1.0 / @k }
      else
        probabilities.map {|p| p / sum.to_f }
      end
    end
  end

  def fast_product(rel, inv_cov)
    sum = 0

    inv_cov.column_count.times do |j|
      local_sum = 0
      (0 ... rel.size).each do |k|
```

```
      local_sum += rel[k] * inv_cov[k, j]
    end
    sum += local_sum * rel[j]
  end

  sum
  end
end
```

The first part iterates through all classes, which holds on to the means and covariances of each cluster. From there, we want to find the inverse covariance matrix as well as the determinant of the covariance. For each row, we calculate a value that is proportional to the probability that the row is in a cluster:

$$p_{ij} = det(C)e^{-\frac{1}{2}\left(x_j - \mu_i\right)C^{-1}\left(x_j - \mu_i\right)}$$

This is effectively a *Gaussian distance metric* to help us determine how far outside the mean our data is.

Let's say that the row vector is exactly the mean. That would mean that this would reduce to $p_{ij} = det(C)$, which is just the determinant of the covariance matrix. This is actually the highest value you can get out of this function. If, for instance, the row vector was far away from the mean vector, then p_{ij} would become smaller and smaller due to the exponentiation and negative fraction in the front.

The nice thing is that this is proportional to the Gaussian probability that the row vector is in the mean. Because this is proportional (not equal), we end up normalizing to sum to 1.

You'll notice one last thing here: the introduction of the `fast_product` method. This is because the Matrix library in Ruby is slow and builds `Array` within `Array`, which is memory inefficient. In this case, things won't change, so we optimized things for that.

Now we can move on to the maximization step:

```
# lib/em_clusterer.rb

class EMClusterer
  # initialize
  # setup_cluster!
  # expect
  # fast_product

  def maximize
    @classes.each_with_index do |klass, i|
      puts "Maximizing for class #{i}"
      sum = Array.new(@width) { 0 }
      num = 0
```

```
@data.each_with_index do |row, j|
  p = @labels[j][i]

  @width.times do |k|
    sum[k] += p * @data[j,k]
  end

  num += p
end

mean = sum.map {|s| s / num }
covariance = Matrix.zero(@width, @width)

@data.row_vectors.each_with_index do |row, j|
  p = @labels[j][i]
  rel = row - Vector[*mean]
  covariance += Matrix.build(@width, @width) do |m,n|
    rel[m] * rel[n] * p
  end
end

covariance = (1.0 / num) * covariance

@classes[i][:means] = Vector[*mean]
@classes[i][:covariance] = covariance
      end
    end
  end
```

Again, here we are iterating over the clusters called @classes. We first make an array called sum, which holds on to the weighted sum of the data happening. From there, we normalize to build a weighted mean. To calculate the covariance matrix, we start with a zero matrix that is square and the width of our clusters. We then iterate through all row_vectors and incrementally add on the weighted difference of the row and the mean for each combination of the matrix. Again, at this point, we normalize and store.

Now we can get down to actually using this. To do that, we add two convenience methods that help in querying the data:

```
# lib/em_clusterer.rb

class EMClusterer
  # initialize
  # setup_cluster!
  # expect
  # fast_product
  # maximize

  def cluster(iterations = 5)
```

```
    iterations.times do |i|
      puts "Iteration #{i}"
      expect_maximize
    end
  end

  def expect_maximize
    expect
    maximize
  end
end
```

EM Jazz Clustering Results

Back to our results using EM clustering with our jazz music. To actually perform the analysis, we run the following script:

```
data = []

artists = []

CSV.foreach('./annotated_jazz_albums.csv', :headers => true) do |row|
  @headers ||= row.headers[2..-1]
  artists << row['artist_album']
  data << row.to_h.values[2..-1].map(&:to_i)
end

data = Matrix[*data]


e = EMClusterer.new(25, data)
e.cluster
```

The first thing you'll notice about EM clustering is that it's slow. It's not as quick as calculating new centroids and iterating. It has to calculate covariances and means, which are inefficient. Occam's Razor would tell us here that most likely EM clustering is not a good use for grouping big amounts of data.

The other thing you'll notice is that our annotated jazz music will not work; this is because the covariance matrix is singular. This is not a good thing. Realistically, this problem is ill suited for EM clustering for this reason, so we have to transform it into a different problem altogether.

We do that by collapsing the dimensions into the top two genres by index:

```
require 'csv'

CSV.open('./less_covariance_jazz_albums.csv', 'wb') do |csv|
  csv << %w[artist_album key_index year].concat(2.times.map {|a| "Genre_#{a}" })

  CSV.foreach('./annotated_jazz_albums.csv', :headers => true) do |row|
    genre_count = 0
```

```
genres = Array.new(2) { 0 }
genre_idx = 0

row.to_h.values[4..-1].each_with_index do |g, i|
  break if genre_idx == 2
  if g == '1'
    genres[genre_idx] = i
    genre_idx += 1
  end
end

next if genres.count {|a| a == 0 } == genres.length

csv << [row['artist_album'], row['key_index'], row['year']].concat(genres)
  end
end
```

Here we're basically saying, for the first two Genres let's assign a genre index and store it. The next problem is that some albums have zero information assigned to them, so we skip those.

At this point, we are able to run the EM Clustering algorithm, except that things become too difficult to actually cluster. This is an important lesson with EM clustering. The data we have actually doesn't cluster because the matrix has become too unstable to invert. I will leave this as an exercise for you to try out to see where it fails, but the covariance matrix just becomes impossible to invert.

Conclusion

Clustering is useful, but because it is unsupervised, it can be a bit hard to control. Coupled with the fact that we are dealing with the impossibility of having consistency, richness, and scale invariance all at once, this means clustering can be a bit useless in many contexts. But don't let that get you down: clustering can be useful for analyzing data sets and splitting data into arbitrary clusters. If you don't care how they are split and just want them split up, then clustering is useful. Just be aware that there are sometimes odd circumstances.

## CHAPTER 9

Kernel Ridge Regression

Regression is probably one of the most ubiquitous tools in any machine learning toolkit. The idea is simple: fit a line to some data mapped from X to Y. You have probably seen lots of regressions already. In many ways, regression models the most common case and our naive base case. As you will see in this chapter, linear regression is a good starting point for predicting data but breaks down quickly when you're trying to model data that has a low number of data points, or that isn't linear.

We will first introduce the problem of collaborative filtering and recommendation algorithms, and then refine how we approach the problem until we reach ridge regression. Finally, at the end of the chapter, we will code our results and figure out whether our assumptions are correct.

 Regression, and by proxy the Kernel Ridge Regression algorithm, is a supervised learning method. It has little restriction on what it can solve but prefers to use continuous variables. It also has the benefit of evening out data and glossing over outliers.

Collaborative Filtering

If you use Amazon to buy things, then you have seen collaborative filtering in action. In Amazon's case, it wants to recommend products of interest to you so that you end up buying more. So, for instance, if you buy lots of beer, then a good recommendation would be some beer for your consumption.

But where collaborative filtering becomes more interesting is how it relates to other users. Given the fact that you are a beer drinker, you might also like kegs, glasses, or even a set of coasters. Even though you haven't actually bought any of those items, other users like you (beer drinkers) have bought them, so most likely you'd like them too.

Graphically collaborative filtering looks something like Figure 9-1.

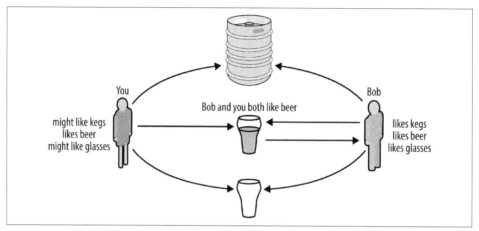

Figure 9-1. You and Bob share a love of beer, therefore you might also like kegs and glasses

There are generally two parts to all collaborative filtering problems:

- Find users who share the same tastes as you (e.g., find other beer drinkers).
- Use the ratings from those like-minded users to make recommendations.

And we take these three approaches to tackle these problems:

- Brute force, a naive approach that will become exponentially slower over time
- *K*-Nearest Neighbors search, which you learned about in Chapter 2
- Regression

Brute force is really the base case. We could iterate through all possible connections and somehow yield the optimal recommendation for the user, but given the fact that the user will most likely want lots of recommendations on every page, this will prove to be slow. The *K*-Nearest Neighbors search would work well. It's lazy, so it wouldn't require a lot of up-front cost, but at the same time, you are making an assumption about the data and there isn't much you can determine about a user from a KNN search except that he is like other users.

Last, we have regression, which would yield a line that fits features to whether the user would like a product or not. The benefit here is that we could determine what a user likes based on the coefficients of the regression as well as use matrix algebra to quickly compute answers. This is probably the best bet, and it's also simple.

Linear Regression Applied to Collaborative Filtering

You have probably heard of linear regression. The idea is simple: given a data set, fit the best line that approximates that data. For instance, let's imagine that we wanted to predict weight given a height. We conceptually know that weight and height are correlated at least (see Figure 9-2). We're using the data of all 11,000 athletes who competed in the 2012 London Olympics (*http://thoughtfulml.com/resources/olympics.csv*).

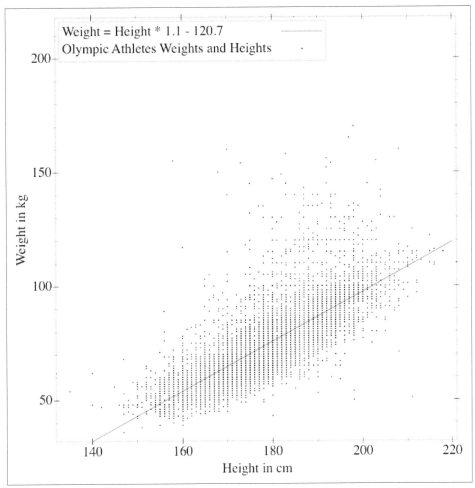

Figure 9-2. Weight as a function of height (we can fit a line that more or less follows the data)

This makes sense: if I am 5'6" (or 1.68 meters) tall, then most likely I will weigh below 200 lbs (91 kg). On the other hand, if I am 6'8" (2.03 meters) tall, then I probably weigh over 250 lbs (113.4 kg). Of course, this is glossing over a lot of outliers, but that's OK! The whole point of regressions is to *regress to the mean*; the line that ends up being drawn is actually the mean of the data points in a lot of cases. Now to get into some technical detail, linear regression's main goal is to minimize the square errors of data—namely, to:

$$\min \Sigma_i^n (\hat{y} - y)^2$$

where $\hat{y}$ is what we get out of our regression model. A linear regression case would take the form of $\hat{y} = \alpha + \beta_1 x_1 + \beta_2 x_2 + \cdots + \beta_n x_n$. Those βs are just coefficients that we find by minimizing the preceding function.

The real power of linear regression models is that to find the coefficients β you need only to do a simple transformation of the original matrix to achieve all of the coefficients.

Using something called the *Moore-Penrose pseudoinverse*, we can actually achieve the answer to the previous optimization problem using the following formula:

$$\vec{\beta} = \left(X^T X\right)^{-1} X^T y$$

Basically, all we need to do is take a transpose (i.e., change the *i,j* element of the matrix to the *j,i* element) of the training data X and multiply it by itself, X. This will always yield a square matrix and then we can invert that using a matrix inverse (I won't get into how to do this, as it's beyond the scope of this book). Finally, we multiply that by the transpose again. This yields a vector of coefficients that best matches the data.

A really nice part of this formula is that you effectively get a mean answer for your data. Let's assume that we have a one-dimensional problem, which is to find a point that is most optimal, and say our data points are 1,2,3,4,5,6. Well, we can map this to a two-dimensional problem by simply saying that $X = 1$ for all points and Y equals 1 through 6. What do we find for a beta when we have this problem?

```
require 'matrix'

y = Matrix[[1],[2],[3],[4],[5],[6]]
x = Matrix[[1],[1],[1],[1],[1],[1]]

(x.transpose * x).inverse * x.transpose * y #=> Matrix[[7/2]]
```

This gives us the mean! So, again, that is all linear regression is doing: regressing to a mean.

A big problem with linear regression, though, is that the matrix multiplied by its transpose will sometimes be singular (meaning it is not invertible). Singular matrices are also called `ill_conditioned` because there just isn't enough data to yield a justified answer to any equation. They are matrices that have a determinant of 0.

More concretely, it looks like this in Ruby code:

```
require 'matrix'

y = Matrix[[1],[2]]

ill_conditioned = Matrix[[1,2,3,4,5,6,7,8,9,10], [10,9,8,7,6,5,4,3,2,1]]
(ill_conditioned.transpose * ill_conditioned).singular? #=> true
(ill_conditioned.transpose * ill_conditioned).inverse #=> Throws an error

conditioned = Matrix[[1,2], [2,1]]
(conditioned.transpose * conditioned).inverse * conditioned.transpose * y #=> Matrix[[(1/1)], [(0/1)]]
```

What this shows you is that if, for instance, you have a lot of variables like the first `ill_conditioned` problem, then there is no suitable way to solve this problem using linear regression because there aren't enough data points to find the optimal minimized least squares. The inner matrix will become singular when there are more features than there are data points.

But let's think about this problem a little more.

Introducing Regularization, or Ridge Regression

Our `ill_conditioned` regression problem is recapped in Table 9-1.

Table 9-1. Ill_conditioned problem

Y	X₁	X₂	X₃	X₄	X₅	X₆	X₇	X₈	X₉	X₁₀
1	1	2	3	4	5	6	7	8	9	10
2	10	9	8	7	6	5	4	3	2	1

Even without any algorithm to solve this, you can see that a lot of the data here is pretty useless. What we are looking for is a function that will yield 1 in the first case and 2 in the second case, so we probably want to find information that is 2× as big in the second case and 1× in the first. That means that columns like X_1, X_2, X_5, X_6, X_9, and X_10 are probably useless. So let's take those out and look again (Table 9-2).

Table 9-2. Ill_conditioned problem with fewer columns

Y	X_3	X_4	X_7	X_8
1	3	4	7	8
2	8	7	4	3

As a matter of fact, X_7 and X_8 are not really needed either, so let's forget about them as well. That leaves us with X_3 and X_4. Now we can actually solve this:

```
require 'matrix'

y = Matrix[[1],[2]]
simplified = Matrix[[3,4], [8,7]]

betas = (simplified.transpose * simplified).inverse * simplified.transpose * y
# => Matrix[[(1/11)], [(2/11)]]
```

This solves the problem! All we did was get rid of the extraneous variables that didn't make a difference. But the question is, can we make this more algorithmic instead of just anecdotal?

Yes, we can—by using something called a *Kernel Ridge Regression*, or *Regularized Regression*.

The basic idea is to introduce a ridge parameter, which will help address the problems with ill_conditioned we have seen before:

```
require 'matrix'
y = Matrix[[1],[2]]
ill_conditioned = Matrix[[1,2,3,4,5,6,7,8,9,10],[10,9,8,7,6,5,4,3,2,1]]

shrinkage = 0.0001

left_half = ill_conditioned.transpose * ill_conditioned + shrinkage * Matrix.ide
ntity(ill_conditioned.column_size)
left_half.singular? #=> false

betas = left_half.inverse * ill_conditioned.transpose * y

betas.transpose * ill_conditioned.row(0) #=> Vector[1.0000000549097194]
betas.transpose * ill_conditioned.row(1) #=> Vector[1.9999994492261521]
```

As you can see, adding in this shrinkage factor has helped us overcome the problem of singular matrices, and we can actually solve this ill-posed problem easily. But there is still one snag we need to deal with: nonlinearity.

Kernel Ridge Regression

As you may recall from Chapter 6, we introduced kernels that would take nonlinear data and transform it into a new feature space where all of a sudden it was linear. Kernels are a powerful tool and well suited for problems in which the data is nonlinear.

To refresh your memory, here are the kernel functions we discussed in Chapter 6:

Homogenous polynomial

$$K\left(x_i, x_j\right) = \left(x_i^T x_j\right)^d$$

Heterogeneous polynomial

$$K\left(x_i, x_j\right) = \left(x_i^T x_j + c\right)^d$$

Radial basis function

$$K\left(x_i, x_j\right) = e^{-\frac{\| \|x_i - x_j\| \|_2^2}{2 * \sigma^2}}$$

The important thing to know here is that we don't actually have to calculate a lot of this, as much of the time these functions are in addition to the part of the regression where X^{XT}. Basically, without getting too deep into the mathematics, we can replace that term with K, which is a kernel representing a new, nonlinear space.

So now our equation looks similar:

$$\hat{y} = y^T (K + \lambda I)^{-1} \kappa$$

$$K_{ij} = f\left(x_i, x_j\right)$$

$$\kappa_i = f\left(x_i, x'\right)$$

This is simply a change. You can just add these functions into the preceding function, and that will effectively turn the regression from linear to having a kernel—very much like how we used them in Chapter 6.

Wrap-Up of Theory

The Kernel Ridge Regressions algorithm can be useful for finding simple functions to map an ill-posed problem. In the next section, we'll see how to actually use this algorithm to recommend beer styles to people based on user preferences expressed in reviews.

Collaborative Filtering with Beer Styles

Remember our collaborative filtering with beer drinkers from earlier in the chapter? What if we were to apply the same to an actual data set—namely, beer styles (*http://bit.ly/1nwvNSI*)? All of the reviewers completed reviews as to whether they liked the taste, appearance, and other attributes of different selections.

Data Set

This data set has beer styles, beers, breweries, reviewers, and reviews. There are 1,586,615 reviews, 62,260 unique beers, 33,388 reviewers, 5,743 breweries, and 104 unique beer styles. Until this point, we've been loading everything into memory and analyzing this way, but this data set is large so a better approach is to load this info into some sort of database.

Setup Notes

All of the code we're using for this example can be found on Git-Hub (*http://bit.ly/Y9xCzg*).

Ruby is constantly changing, so the *README* file is the best place to get up to speed on running the examples.

Why Regression for Collaborative Filtering?

If you have ever read any other books on machine learning or data science, most likely you haven't heard of regression being used for collaborative filtering. In most cases, people will build what is called *matrix factorization* to find recommendations.

We use regression in this example because it is well suited for determining the linear combination of factors that will identify what someone wants. The beauty is that you can use this to figure out someone's preferences. So, for instance, in beer reviews, we can figure out whether someone likes alcohol more than palate. While we can do that with matrix factorization as well, this is slightly different.

The Tools We Will Need

To accomplish our collaborative filtering on beer styles, we need to build some tables into Postgres. I think Sequel is much easier to use than ActiveRecord for small projects like this, so we'll use that.

First, let's define some tables to use and some models. We will need tables for beers, reviews, reviewers, breweries, reviews, and beer styles.

To start out, let's create our file bootstrap, which will make sure the tables exist and everything migrates correctly:

```
# script/load_db.rb

# Note that this doesn't have to be postgres—you can use sqlite or mysql, too

DB = Sequel.connect('postgres://localhost/beer_reviews')

DB.create_table? :beers do
  primary_key :id
  Integer :beer_style_id, :index => true
  Integer :brewery_id, :index => true
  String :name
  Float :abv
end
```

Beers have a *beer_style_id*, *name*, *abv*, and *brewery_id*. We want to make this fairly spread out, so a *beer_style_id* is a foreign key to *beer_styles* that we will make. *abv* is simply alcohol by volume, and lastly, *brewery_id* is a foreign key to breweries. Next, let's build our breweries as well as everything else:

```
# script/load_db.rb

# DB
# create_table :beers

DB.create_table? :breweries do
  primary_key :id
  String :name
end

DB.create_table? :reviewers do
  primary_key :id
  String :name
end

DB.create_table? :reviews do
  primary_key :id
  Integer :reviewer_id, :index => true
  Integer :beer_id, :index => true
  Float :overall
  Float :aroma
  Float :appearance
  Float :palate
  Float :taste
end

DB.create_table? :beer_styles do
  primary_key :id
  String :name, :index => true
end
```

Now we need to load the information, which we can do through the following script:

```ruby
# script/load_db.rb

# DB
# create_table :beers
# create_table :breweries
# create_table :reviewers
# create_table :reviews
# create_table :beer_styles

require 'csv'
require 'set'

# brewery_id,brewery_name,review_time,review_overall,review_aroma,review_appeara
nce,review_profilename,beer_style,review_palate,review_tast,beer_name,beer_abv,b
eer_beerid
breweries = {}
reviewers = {}
beer_styles = {}

if !File.exists?('./beer_reviews/beer_reviews.csv')
  system('bzip2 -cd ./beer_reviews/beer_reviews.csv.bz2 > ./beer_reviews/beer_re
views.csv') or die
end

CSV.foreach('./beer_reviews/beer_reviews.csv', :headers => true) do |line|
  puts line
  if !breweries.has_key?(line.fetch('brewery_name'))
    b = Brewery.create(:name => line.fetch('brewery_name'))
    breweries[line.fetch('brewery_name')] = b.id
  end

  if !reviewers.has_key?(line.fetch('review_profilename'))
    r = Reviewer.create(:name => line.fetch('review_profilename'))
    reviewers[line.fetch('review_profilename')] = r.id
  end

  if !beer_styles.has_key?(line.fetch('beer_style'))
    bs = BeerStyle.create(:name => line.fetch('beer_style'))
    beer_styles[line.fetch('beer_style')] = bs.id
  end

  beer = Beer.create({
    :beer_style_id => beer_styles.fetch(line.fetch('beer_style')),
    :name => line.fetch('beer_name'),
    :abv => line.fetch('beer_abv'),
    :brewery_id => breweries.fetch(line.fetch('brewery_name'))
  })

  Review.create({
    :reviewer_id => reviewers.fetch(line.fetch('review_profilename')),
    :beer_id => beer.id,
```

```
    :overall => line.fetch('review_overall'),
    :aroma => line.fetch('review_aroma'),
    :appearance => line.fetch('review_appearance'),
    :palate => line.fetch('review_palate'),
    :taste => line.fetch('review_taste')
  })
end
```

Now that we have loaded our data, we can move on to testing and building our recommendation algorithm using Ridge Regression.

Reviewer

Our first step is to quickly put together associations between all models, and to do that we write the following:

```
# lib/models/reviewer.rb

class Reviewer < Sequel::Model
  one_to_many :reviews
  one_to_many :user_preferences
end

# lib/models/brewery.rb
class Brewery < Sequel::Model
  one_to_many :beers
end

# lib/models/beer_style.rb
class BeerStyle < Sequel::Model
  one_to_many :beers
end

# lib/models/review.rb
class Review < Sequel::Model
  many_to_one :reviewer
end

# lib/models/user_preference.rb
class UserPreference < Sequel::Model
  many_to_one :reviewer
  many_to_one :beer_style
end
```

At this point, we need to build a test for two different scenarios. The first is that for each rated style we want to assign a nonzero constant. The second is that we want the highest slope to be the most favorite style, and we want the smallest slope to be the least liked beer style.

To test for a correct calculation, we write the following:

```
# test/lib/models/reviewer_spec.rb
describe Reviewer do
  let(:reviewer) { Reviewer.find(:id => 3) }

  it 'calculates a preference for a user correctly' do
    pref = reviewer.preference

    reviewed_styles = reviewer.reviews.map {|r| r.beer.beer_style_id }

    pref.each_with_index do |r,i|
      if reviewed_styles.include?(i + 1)
        r.wont_equal 0
      else
        r.must_equal 0
      end
    end
  end
end
```

Let's just assume that you have loaded `Reviewer` into the database and that you can pick a random reviewer to test, like id = 3. This test will make sure that there is only 0s for styles not rated, and a nonzero constant for rated styles.

From here, we can test the real question, which is whether we can come up with a ranking for beer style likes. We do this by writing the following test:

```
# test/lib/models/reviewer_spec.rb

describe Reviewer do
  let (:reviewer) { Reviewer.find(:id => 3) }

  # Test from above

  it 'gives the highest rated beer_style the highest constant' do
    pref = reviewer.preference

    most_liked = pref.index(pref.max) + 1

    least_liked = pref.index(pref.select(&:nonzero?).min) + 1

    reviews = {}
    reviewer.reviews.each do |r|
      reviews[r.beer.beer_style_id] ||= []
      reviews[r.beer.beer_style_id] << r.overall
    end

    review_ratings = Hash[reviews.map {|k,v| [k, v.inject(&:+) / v.length.to_
f] }]

    assert review_ratings.fetch(most_liked) > review_ratings.fetch(least_liked)
```

```
    best_fit = review_ratings.max_by(&:last)
    worst_fit = review_ratings.min_by(&:last)

    assert best_fit.first == most_liked || best_fit.last == review_ratings[most_
liked]
    assert worst_fit.first == least_liked || worst_fit.last == review_ratings[le
ast_liked]
  end
end
```

Now, of course, we need to write the actual code to make this work.

Writing the Code to Figure Out Someone's Preference

The problem we are trying to solve with these two tests is really finding a linear combination of beer styles to average ratings overall. There are around 104 beer styles, and most users won't review that often. Therefore, we will probably have singular matrices, and regression won't work right out of the box. So instead, we have to build an algorithm that will shrink the matrix enough so that it can invert. We do this by exponentially increasing the shrinkage parameter until it works.

You will notice that I am using the NMatrix library, which is a subset of NArray. This is purely for speed. Unfortunately, the Matrix library in Ruby is slow and inefficient, so to do lots of calculations we have to utilize NMatrix. There are downsides to this library too, though, which are that NMatrix is really just a simple hack on top of NArray and doesn't have features like determinants or other neat tools. So I created a class called MatrixDeterminance that takes a matrix and calculates its determinant:

```
# lib/matrix_determinance.rb

require 'narray'
require 'nmatrix'

class MatrixDeterminance
  def initialize(matrix)
    @matrix = matrix
  end

  def determinant
    raise "Must be square" unless square?
    size = @matrix.sizes[1]
    last = size - 1
    a = @matrix.to_a
    no_pivot = Proc.new{ return 0 }
    sign = +1
    pivot = 1.0
    size.times do |k|
      previous_pivot = pivot
      if (pivot = a[k][k].to_f).zero?
```

```
          switch = (k+1 ... size).find(no_pivot) {|row|
            a[row][k] != 0
          }
          a[switch], a[k] = a[k], a[switch]
          pivot = a[k][k]
          sign = -sign
        end
        (k+1).upto(last) do |i|
          ai = a[i]
          (k+1).upto(last) do |j|
            ai[j] = (pivot * ai[j] - ai[k] * a[k][j]) / previous_pivot
          end
        end
      end
      sign * pivot
    end

    def singular?
      determinant == 0
    end

    def square?
      @matrix.sizes[0] == @matrix.sizes[1]
    end

    def regular?
      !singular?
    end
  end
```

The way to use this is simple: just initialize a new `MatrixDeterminance` object and you can calculate whether that matrix is singular or regular and what the determinant is.

Now we can calculate the user's preference using a ridge regression:

```
# lib/models/reviewer.rb

class Reviewer < Sequel::Model
  one_to_many :reviews
  one_to_many :user_preferences

  IDENTITY = NMatrix[
    *Array.new(104) { |i|
      Array.new(104) { |j|
        (i == j) ? 1.0 : 0.0
      }
    }
  ]

  def preference
    @max_beer_id = BeerStyle.count
    return [] if reviews.empty?
```

```
rows = []
overall = []

context = DB.fetch(<<-SQL)
  SELECT
    AVG(reviews.overall) AS overall
    , beers.beer_style_id AS beer_style_id
  FROM reviews
  JOIN beers ON beers.id = reviews.beer_id
  WHERE reviewer_id = #{self.id}
  GROUP BY beer_style_id;
SQL

context.each do |review|
  overall << review.fetch(:overall)
  beers = Array.new(@max_beer_id) { 0 }
  beers[review.fetch(:beer_style_id) - 1] = 1
  rows << beers
end

x = NMatrix[*rows]
shrinkage = 0

left = nil
iteration = 6

xtx = (x.transpose * x).to_f

left = xtx + shrinkage * IDENTITY

until MatrixDeterminance.new(left).regular?
  puts "Shrinking iteration #{iteration}"
  shrinkage = (2 ** iteration) * 10e-6

  (left * x.transpose * NMatrix[overall].transpose).to_a.flatten
end
  end
  end
```

You can see that this is a pretty fat method, but let's go through it together. The first step is to find what the maximum beer_style_id is. Our eventual vector will be this wide. Next, we set up a context, which is simply the average review for each reviewed beer style. We then set the reviewed beer_style_ids to 1.

Finally, we get into the actual regression problem, which is where we are trying to map overall review to the beer styles. From here, we iterate the shrinkage parameter until the matrix is invertible so we can actually regress. Finally, we find the slope parameters and return that.

You are probably wondering what we can do with this. It is just a slope of how much someone likes a beer. We can persist this preference by storing it in the table user_preferences. This would be a `beer_style_id` and a preference. From that table we can then graphically move from top preferences to other reviewers who reviewed the same beer and liked it.

This is a form of collaborative filtering. We have identified the preference of the user, and using that, we can move in a graph to the next user.

Collaborative Filtering with User Preferences

To achieve what is effectively a form of collaborative filtering, we want to find users who have similar taste and then find out what they like that we haven't tried yet. To make this work in code, we would do the following:

```ruby
# lib/models/reviewer.rb

class Reviewer < Sequel::Model
  def friend
    skip_these = styles_tasted - [favorite.id]

    someone_else = UserPreference.where(
      'beer_style_id = ? AND beer_style_id NOT IN ? AND reviewer_id != ?',
      favorite.id,
      skip_these,
      self.id
    ).order(:preference).last.reviewer
  end

  def styles_tasted
    reviews.map { |r| r.beer.beer_style_id }.uniq
  end

  def recommend_new_style
    UserPreference.where(
      'beer_style_id NOT IN ? AND reviewer_id = ?',
      styles_tasted,
      friend.id
    ).order(:preference).last.beer_style
  end
end
```

This yields a method, `recommend_new_style`, that will tell us a new style to taste. The best part about this is that we don't really need to test explicitly because we have already tested the preference. That's all we need.

Conclusion

The Kernel Ridge Regression algorithm is a useful tool to find quick solutions to problems that are ill posed—that is, if the x variable is higher than the actual observations. This happens a lot with reviews; users get bored and want to move on. While you could use other methods, a Ridge Regression will work perfectly fine.

As you saw, Ridge Regressions are powerful: we found a preference of beer styles and implemented a collaborative filter of sorts. After calculating the preference, the algorithm can find a similar preference and make recommendations to us from that.

## CHAPTER 10

Improving Models and Data Extraction

Sometimes, no matter how good an algorithm is, it just doesn't work. Or worse, it doesn't pick up anything. Data can be quite noisy, and sometimes it's just about impossible to figure out what went wrong. This chapter focuses on improving what you already have by either selecting better features, or transforming your features into a new set. We do this by monitoring metrics as they relate to either cross-validations or production monitoring.

This chapter will be somewhat of a smorgasbord when it comes to improving your models. That is because there are many ways of fixing models.

The Problem with the Curse of Dimensionality

As we've talked about before, the curse of dimensionality is a big problem with distance-based machine learning algorithms. Generally speaking, as the number of dimensions increases, the average distance also goes up. Take, for instance, the case in Figure 10-1, where we see a perfect sphere centered at 0,0,0.

Everything is fine in three dimensions, but what if we project only onto two dimensions? What ends up happening is quite illuminating (see Figure 10-2).

In these figures, you'll see a unit sphere on the left. This unit sphere was created using random points along the outer edge. On the right, you see a circle, but it is in fact the same sphere projected onto a two-dimensional space. In the first case, the sphere is a unit, so the distance to the edge is exactly 1, whereas the average in the circle is 0.74. This means that as you project onto fewer and fewer dimensions, the distances become shorter. We have already solved this in Chapter 3 (the *K*-Nearest Neighbors chapter) by introducing SURF for feature extraction. Instead of trying to find the nearest neighbor of all pixels, we needed to use a smaller data set. As we know, the only way of getting over the curse is to reduce the dimensions.

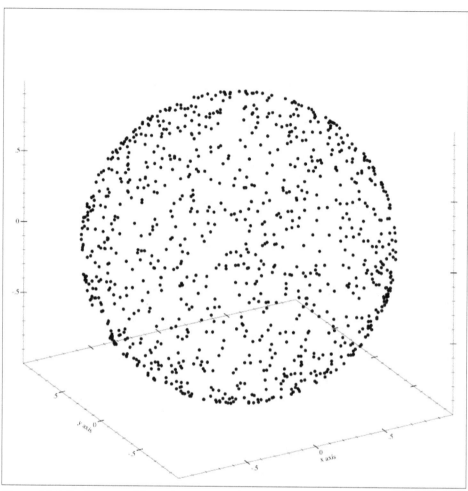

Figure 10-1. In the case of three dimensions, the average distance is 1 because it is perfect

In this section, we will discuss two different methods of overcoming the curse of dimensionality: feature selection and feature transformation.

Feature Selection

Let's think about some data that doesn't make a whole lot of sense. Let's say that we want to measure weather data and want to be able to predict temperature given three variables: coffee consumption, ice cream consumption, and season. See Table 10-1.

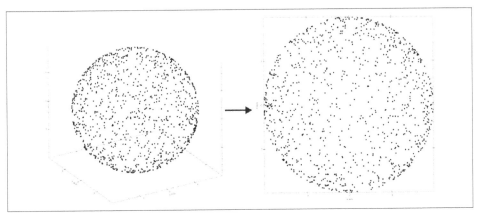

Figure 10-2. In this case of dimension = 2, the average distance is 0.74

Table 10-1. Weather data for Seattle as related to Matt's ice cream and coffee consumption

Average temperature	Matt's coffee consumption	Matt's ice cream consumption	Month
47F	4	2	Jan
50F	4	2	Feb
54F	4	3	Mar
58F	4	3	Apr
65F	4	3	May
70F	4	3	Jun
76F	4	4	Jul
76F	4	4	Aug
71F	4	4	Sep
60F	4	3	Oct
51F	4	2	Nov
46F	4	2	Dec

You can see that I generally drink about four cups of coffee a day. I tend to eat more ice cream in the summer, and it's generally hotter around that time (Figure 10-3).

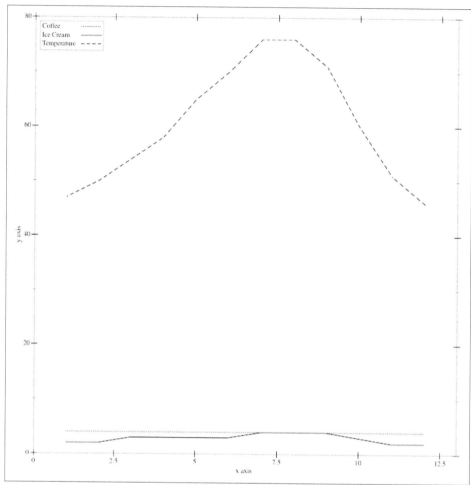

Figure 10-3. A graph showing my ice cream consumption

Now we know inherently that the one thing that causes temperature changes is the season. It is generally hotter during the summer, and cooler during the winter. That is because the sun is in a different place in the sky. Ice cream consumption doesn't matter and neither does coffee consumption. Ice cream consumption does correlate with the hotter months.

The thing to realize here, though, is that we have one feature that is irrelevant and will just skew data toward it; we have a composed variable, which is really a combination of other variables outside our model; and finally we have a signal, which is the month, however.

Say, for instance, we wanted to take a random subset of variables and test whether that improved our data. We can do that. This is called *random feature selection*, and it actually ends up working a lot of the time. The reason usually has to do with data being better behaved in smaller dimensions. So even though we're randomly reducing dimensions, we are improving our data.

The basic idea is to take a random subset of data and to run your model against it then. Random feature selection is probably one of the simplest model improvement tools out there.

But there is one big downside to doing this, and that is slowness. Unfortunately, wrapping a model with some feature selection will take a long time. That is because you need to take data randomly, select a subset and run your model, and then test its fitness. As you might expect, this will take a long time to achieve. But in the case of K-Nearest Neighbors or other fast algorithms, this might be good enough. But what if you were to give a Neural Network better data or something that might take some time? For that, we can filter our data even before it gets sent to the algorithm.

Feature Transformation

To understand feature transformation, let's think about the case of keeping a food journal. A lot of us diet and track calories. Let's just say you want to track when you are hungry versus when you are not. So you keep a log of what hour of the day it is and how hungry you are.

The only problem is that you traveled between Los Angeles and Hawaii during the time you logged your hunger. The data you have collected is shown in Table 10-2.

Table 10-2. Hunger log

Hungry?	Hour of day	Timezone offset
Yes	7	−8
No	8	−10
No	9	−8
Yes	9	−10
Yes	12	−8
No	14	−10
No	15	−8
No	16	−8

Hungry?	Hour of day	Timezone offset
No	18	−10
No	19	−10
Yes	18	−8
Yes	20	−10

This data would yield a noisy look into when you get hungry, as Figure 10-4 illustrates.

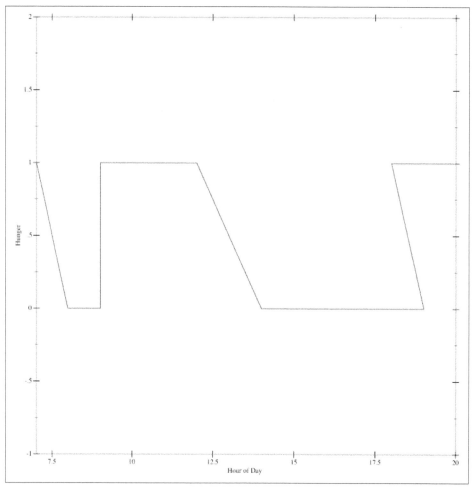

Figure 10-4. Not a very definite trend

You can see that there doesn't seem to be any sort of pattern to your eating. You're just kind of hungry or not.

But if you instead group the hour of day and timezone offset together in a linear combination, you'll notice that in fact you get hungry three times a day: at 7, 12, and 6. You'd get something completely different that looks like Figure 10-5.

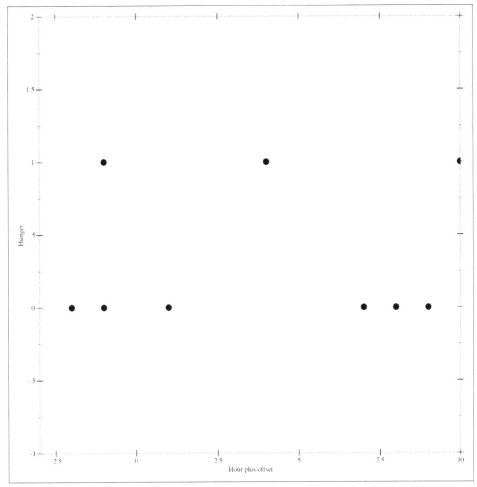

Figure 10-5. Transformed to sum offset and hour of day

There is a better way of doing this, which is through *feature transformation algorithms*. There are a bunch of different types, but we're going to focus on PCA and ICA.

Principal Component Analysis (PCA)

Principal Component Analysis has been around for a long time. This algorithm simply looks at the direction with the most variance and then determines that as the first principal component. This is very similar to how regression works in that it determines the best direction to map data to. Imagine you have a noisy data set that looks like Figure 10-6.

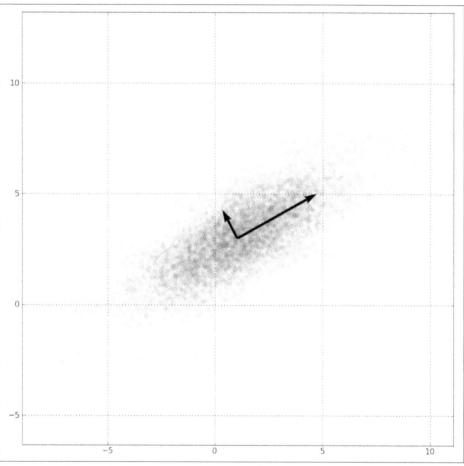

Figure 10-6. Principal components in the scatterplot

As you can see, the data has a definite direction: up and to the right. If we were to determine the principal component, it would be that direction because the data is in maximal variance that way. The second principal component would end up being orthogonal to that, and then over iterations we would reduce our dimensions by transforming them into these principal directions.

Another way of thinking about PCA is how it relates to faces. When you apply PCA to a set of faces, an odd result happens known as the Eigenfaces (see Figure 10-7).

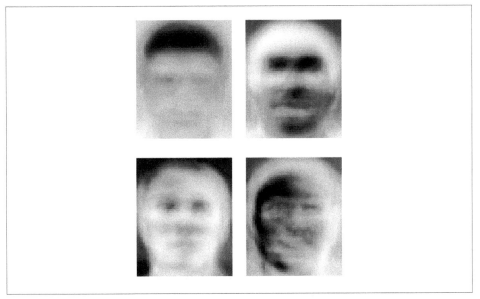

Figure 10-7. Eigenfaces from AT&T Laboratories, Cambridge

While these look quite odd, it is fascinating that what comes out is really an average face summed up over all of the training data. Instead of implementing PCA now, we'll wait until the next section where we implement ICA—which actually relies on PCA as well.

Independent Component Analysis (ICA)

Imagine you are at a party and your friend is coming over to talk to you. Near you is someone you hate who won't shut up, and on the other side of the room is a washing machine that keeps making noise (see Figure 10-8).

You want to know what your friend has been up to, so you listen to her closely. Being human, you are adept at separating out sounds like the washing machine and that loud mouth you hate. But how could we do that with data?

Let's say that instead of listening to your friend, you only had a recording and wanted to filter out all of the noise in the background. How would you do something like that? You'd use an algorithm called Independent Component Analysis.

Technically, ICA minimizes mutual information, or the information shared between the two variables. Intuitively, this makes sense: find me the signals in the aggregate that are different.

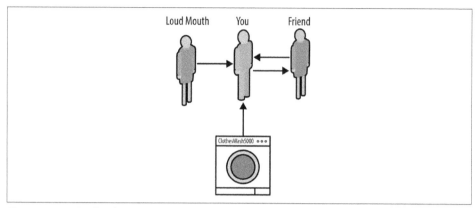

Figure 10-8. Cocktail party example

Compared to our face recognition example in Figure 10-7, what does ICA extract? Well, unlike Eigenfaces, it extracts features of a face, like noses, eyes, and hair.

Both algorithms are useful for transforming data and can analyze information even more (see Figure 10-9).

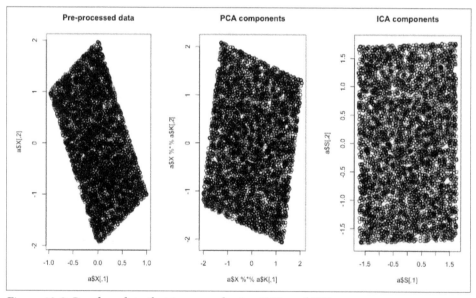

Figure 10-9. Random data that is mapped using PCA and ICA

Unfortunately, as with PCA, there is no Ruby gem for ICA. Instead, we can rely on the "R in Ruby" gem to call into R. This is definitely cheating for a book on using machine learning in Ruby, but sometimes it is perfectly useful to call out to other languages. Another possibility would be to use JRuby and utilize FastICA, which is actually what gets used in R as well.

Setup Notes

To get these examples running, check out this book's examples on GitHub (*http://bit.ly/1ulTwKd*).

You will have to install R to get this to work properly.

The first step we need to take is to install FastICA in R. We can do that by typing the following:

```
# example_1.rb

require 'rinruby'

R.eval(<<-R)
  install.packages("fastICA")
  library(fastICA)
  S <- matrix(runif(10000), 5000, 2)
  A <- matrix(c(1, 1, -1, 3), 2, 2, byrow = TRUE)
  X <- S %*% A
  a <- fastICA(X, 2, alg.typ = "parallel", fun = "logcosh", alpha = 1,
  method = "C", row.norm = FALSE, maxit = 200,
  tol = 0.0001, verbose = TRUE)
  par(mfrow = c(1, 3))
  plot(a$X, main = "Pre-processed data")
  plot(a$X %*% a$K, main = "PCA components")
  plot(a$S, main = "ICA components")
R
```

Now that we know about feature transformation, feature selection, and more, let's get into the last part of this chapter, which is monitoring performance of machine learning in a production environment.

Monitoring Machine Learning Algorithms

Throughout the book we've talked about writing tests, cross-validation, and Occam's Razor, but little about monitoring the code. If production code seems fine, then you aren't measuring enough. When it comes to machine learning, things are no different: just because these algorithms can seem magical at times doesn't mean that we can just deploy without continually testing our code.

The tools we can use are generally measuring precision and recall and alerting us when anomalies happen. We will also discuss an online way to measure mean squared error.

Precision and Recall: Spam Filter

Remember our spam filter? In short, we wanted to mark email as either spam or ham. Since email is important, we talked about the notion that we would rather have less precision—meaning some spam messages make it into our inbox—than to miss an important message that was mistakenly marked as spam.

Let's say that we have found that the data in Table 10-3 is true.

Table 10-3. Spam versus ham based on experience

	Predicted ham	Predicted spam
Ham	10,000	100
Spam	40	60

Looking at this, we are correctly calculating that 10,000 ham messages are in fact ham. Unfortunately, 100 of the actual ham messages were classified as spam.

This is useful information, and when we cross-validated, we used this to optimize our model. But what if we wanted to monitor this? That is where precision, accuracy, and recall come in (see Figure 10-10).

Precision is the amount of correctly classified spam divided by the predicted spam. That would be 60/160 or 3/8. This is bad. What this means is that the algorithm gives us more irrelevant examples for spam. So it thinks that ham is actually spam when it isn't.

Accuracy is the correctly classified examples divided by the total amount of examples used. So in this case, it would be (10,000 + 60) / (10,000 + 100 + 40 + 60), or roughly 98.6%. This isn't too bad; it means that 98.6% of the examples are correct. We have used this throughout the book, extensively measuring error rates.

Lastly, we have *recall*, which is 60 / (60 + 40) or 3/5. This means that we got more than half of the spam examples, which is good.

These metrics are useful inside of cross-validations, but I find them much better suited for monitoring. It's important to measure all of these as users interact and feed more data into the algorithm.

So, for instance, let's say that our spam filter really doesn't work well and people keep marking new things as spam when it was ham. What would that do to our metrics? See Table 10-4 for the answer.

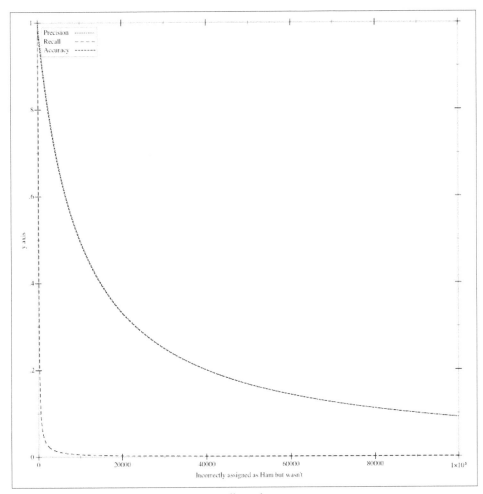

Figure 10-10. The decay of precision, recall, and accuracy

Table 10-4. Data supporting graph

Predicted as ham but isn't	Ham precision	Recall	Accuracy
0	100%	100%	99%
10	99%	85%	98.9%
20	99%	75%	98%
30	99.7%	66%	98%
..	..	..	..

Predicted as ham but isn't	Ham precision	Recall	Accuracy
60	99.4%	50%	98%
..	..	..	..
100	99%	37.5%	98%

As you can see, false negatives will have little impact on a problem with lots of training in terms of accuracy, but when it comes to recall it will. When recall dips below 50%, the model becomes less viable, and monitoring alerts should be generated.

The Confusion Matrix

We've been talking about false and positive predictions, but there is a more general term for this: the *confusion matrix*. This term relates to correctly classified instances. So, for example, let's say we classify into three beer categories: Pilsner, Stout, and Hefeweizen. And given our classification algorithm, we found the data shown in Table 10-5.

Table 10-5. Confusion matrix

	Pilsner	Stout	Hefeweizen
Pilsner	20	1	3
Stout	1	30	1
Hefeweizen	5	1	10

These are different beers, so our algorithm found a decent classification of the examples. From this confusion matrix, you can calculate the recalls, precision, and overall accuracy of the model.

For instance, the precision of Stout is 30/32, or around 93%. The recall of Stout is also 30/32.

Unfortunately, confusion matrices have one downside—they only work with discrete classification problems. What about something like a regression or an algorithm that returns a continuous variable? For that, we have to rely on mean squared error.

Mean Squared Error

When it comes to measuring an algorithm, like predictions of a continuous variable such as a review, we need to take a different approach, which is to measure the mean squared error of the model. But that is difficult to do in a production context because you'd have to keep around all past classifications and errors. Actually, not so! There is a workaround.

Say our goal is to measure mean squared error over time as new information comes in. Let's say we have a model:

$$\hat{y} = f(x)$$

where y is some real number. Assuming we can get some information from our users, like what they'd actually rate whatever it is, we could then determine an error:

$$\epsilon = (\hat{y} - y)^2$$

We square the error mainly to make it positive.

This is where most people would think that you would have to hold on to all errors and calculate:

$$\Sigma_{i=0}^{n} \epsilon_i$$

But we can calculate an incremental squared error instead. First, let's rewrite this as the following:

$$\overline{\epsilon_n} = \frac{\epsilon_1 + \epsilon_2 + \cdots + \epsilon_n}{n}$$

Likewise, we can say the next average will equal the following:

$$\overline{\epsilon_{n+1}} = \frac{\epsilon_1 + \epsilon_2 + \cdots + \epsilon_n + \epsilon_{n+1}}{n+1}$$

Now if we multiply the first equation by n, we can actually just input that into the fraction. So:

$$\overline{\epsilon_{n+1}} = \frac{n^{\star}\overline{\epsilon_n} + \epsilon_{n+1}}{n+1}$$

This means that the next average is simply the previous average multiplied by the amount of used instances divided by the new instances:

So let's say that our current mean squared error is 2 calculated over 10 iterations. We find out in iteration 11 that the squared error was 100. That means that the new average should equal (2 * 10 + 100)/11, which equals around 10.9.

This means that we can easily build a program that monitors mean squared error in production.

```ruby
# incremental_meaner.rb

class IncrementalMeaner
  attr_reader :current_mean, :n
  def initialize
    @current_mean = 0
    @n = 0
    @mutex = Mutex.new
  end

  def add(error)
    @mutex.synchronize {
      @current_mean = (((@n * @current_mean) + error) / (@n + 1.0)
      @n += 1
      @current_mean
    }
  end
end
```

The Wilds of Production Environments

As they say, anything that can go wrong probably will. This is especially true of production environments. We can cross-validate, test our seams, and determine that our model is good, but when it is in production, it can still break down. User input is one thing that we can't optimize for, because people will do the funniest things. So it's important to build monitoring around mean squared error as well as precision recall metrics to develop more confidence in how the algorithm is performing.

There is also an architectural component to this, which is that there needs to be a feedback loop with algorithms. In other words, there needs to be something to test against. Otherwise, the code will not work and you'll end up with the problem that websites have with poorly trained information that becomes stagnant and useless. In the end, user experience is what we are trying to optimize with machine learning algorithms.

Conclusion

This chapter was kind of a smorgasbord of different ways to improve an existing model. Sometimes you can just select features that work better, and sometimes you need to transform. But the most important part is to make sure that we are measuring our results against a baseline and monitoring success in production or with our users.

## CHAPTER 11

Putting It All Together

Well, here we are! The end of the book. While you probably don't have the same depth of understanding as a PhD in machine learning, I hope you have learned something. Specifically, I hope you've developed a thought process for approaching problems that machine learning works so well at solving. I firmly believe that using tests is the only way that we can effectively use the scientific method. It is the reason the modern world exists, and it helps us become much better at writing code.

Of course, you can't write a test for everything, but it's the mindset that matters. And hopefully you have learned a bit about how you can apply that mindset to machine learning. In this chapter, we will discuss what we covered at a high level, and I'll post some suggested reading for you so you can dive further into machine learning research.

Machine Learning Algorithms Revisited

As we touched on earlier in the book, machine learning is a split into three main categories: supervised, unsupervised, and reinforcement learning (Table 11-1). This book skips reinforcement learning, but I highly suggest you research it now that you have a better background. I'll list a source for you in the final section of this chapter.

Table 11-1. Machine learning categories

Category	Description
Supervised	Supervised learning is the most common machine learning category. This is functional approximation. We are trying to map some data points to some fuzzy function. Optimization wise, we are trying to fit a function that best approximates the data to use in the future. It is called "supervised" because it has a learning set given to it.

Category	Description
Unsupervised	Unsupervised learning is just analyzing data without any sort of Y to map to. It is called "unsupervised" because the algorithm doesn't know what the output should be and instead has to come up with it itself.
Reinforcement	Reinforcement learning is similar to supervised learning, but with a reward that is generated from each step. For instance, this is like a mouse looking for cheese in a maze. The mouse wants to find the cheese and in most cases will not be rewarded until the end when it finally finds it.

There are generally two types of biases for each of these categories. One is the restriction bias and the other is preference. Restriction bias is basically what limits the algorithm, while preference is what sort of problems it prefers.

All of this information (shown in Table 11-2) helps us determine whether we should use each algorithm or not.

Table 11-2. Machine learning algorithm matrix

Algorithm	Type	Class	Restriction bias	Preference bias
KNN	Supervised learning	Instance based	Generally speaking, KNN is good for measuring distance based approximations; it suffers from the curse of dimensionality	Prefers problems that are distance based
Naive Bayes	Supervised learning	Probabilistic	Works on problems where the inputs are independent from each other	Prefers problems where the probability will always be greater than zero for each class
SVM	Supervised Learning	Decision Boundary	Works where there is a definite distinction between two classifications	Prefers binary classification problems
Neural Networks	Supervised Learning	Nonlinear functional approximation	Little restriction bias	Prefers binary inputs
(Kernel) Ridge Regression	Supervised	Regression	Low restriction on problems it can solve	Prefers continuous variables
Hidden Markov Models	Supervised / Unsupervised	Markovian	Generally works well for system information where the Markov assumption holds	Prefers timeseries data and memoryless information

Algorithm	Type	Class	Restriction bias	Preference bias
Clustering	Unsupervised	Clustering	No restriction	Prefers data that is in groupings given some form of distance (Euclidean, Manhattan, or others)
Filtering	Unsupervised	Feature Transformation	No restriction	Prefer data to have lots of variables to filter on

How to Use This Information for Solving Problems

Using the matrix in Table 11-2, we can figure out how to approach a given problem. For instance, if we are trying to solve a problem like determining what neighborhood someone lives in, KNN is a pretty good choice, whereas Naive Bayesian Classification makes absolutely no sense. But Naive Bayesian Classification could determine sentiment or some other type of probability. The Support Vector Machines algorithm works well for problems that are looking at finding a hard split between two pieces of data, and it doesn't suffer from the curse of dimensionality nearly as much. So SVM tends to be good for word problems where there's a lot of features. Neural Networks can solve problems ranging from classifications to driving a car. Kernel Ridge Regression is really just a simple trick to add onto a linear regression toolbelt and can find the mean of a curve. Hidden Markov Models can follow musical scores, tag parts of speech, and work well for other system-like applications.

Clustering is good at grouping data together without any sort of goal. This can be useful for analysis, or just to build a library and store data effectively. Filtering is well suited for overcoming the curse of dimensionality. We saw it used predominantly in Chapter 3 by reducing extracted pixels to features.

What we didn't touch on in the book is that these algorithms are just a starting point. The important thing to realize is that it doesn't matter what you pick; it is what you are trying to solve that matters. That is why we cross-validate, and measure precision, recall, and accuracy. Testing and checking our work every step of the way guarantees that we at least approach better answers.

I encourage you to read more about machine learning models and to think about applying tests to them. Most algorithms have them baked in, which is good, but to write code that learns over time, we mere humans need to be checking our own work as well.

What's Next for You?

This is just the beginning of your journey. Machine learning is a field that is rapidly growing every single year. We are learning how to build robotic self-driving cars using deep learning networks, and how to classify many things like health problems using Restricted Boltzmann Machines. The future is bright for machine learning, and now that you've read this book you are better equipped to learn more about deeper subtopics like reinforcement learning, deep learning, artificial intelligence in general, and more complicated machine learning algorithms.

There is a plethora of information out there for you. Here are a few resources I recommend:

- Peter Flach, *Machine Learning: The Art and Science of Algorithms That Make Sense of Data* (Cambridge, UK: Cambridge University Press, 2012).

- David J. C. MacKay, *Information Theory, Inference, and Learning Algorithms* (Cambridge, UK: Cambridge University Press, 2003).

- Tom Mitchell, *Machine Learning* (New York: McGraw-Hill, 1997).

- Stuart Russell and Peter Norvig, *Artificial Intelligence: A Modern Approach*, 3rd Edition (London: Pearson Education, 2009).

- Toby Segaran, *Programming Collective Intelligence: Building Smart Web 2.0 Applications* (Sebastopol, CA: O'Reilly Media, 2007).

- Richard Sutton and Andrew Barto, *Reinforcement Learning: An Introduction* (Cambridge, MA: MIT Press, 1998).

Beyond those, there's a massive number of videos to check out online, either through online courses or on YouTube. Watching lectures on deep learning is rewarding. Geoffrey Hinton's lectures (*http://videolectures.net/geoffrey_e_hinton/*) are a great place to start, or check out anything done by Andrew Ng, including his Coursera course (*https://www.coursera.org/instructor/~35*).

Now that you know a bit more about machine learning, you can go out and solve problems that are not black and white, but instead involve many shades of gray. Using a test-driven approach, as we have throughout the book, will equip you to see these problems through a scientific lens and to attempt to solve problems not by being true or false but instead by embracing a higher level of accuracy. Machine learning is a fascinating field because it allows you to take two divergent ideas like computer science, which is theoretically sound, and data, which is practically noisy, and zip them together in one beautiful relationship.

Index

About the Author

Matt Kirk is a programmer who doesn't live in the Bay Area. While he's been programming for over 15 years, he still considers himself just a beginner at everything. His love of learning and building tools has fueled his career, which spans finance, startups, diamonds, heavy machinery, and logging. This book is a distillation—not just of machine learning, but also of a curiosity and love of learning in general. He has spoken at many conferences throughout the world and still enjoys programming daily. When he's not writing software, he's most likely learning about something new, whether it's gardening, music, woodworking, or how to change brake rotors.

Colophon

The animal on the cover of *Thoughtful Machine Learning* is a Eurasian eagle-owl (*Bubo bubo*), which is found, as its name suggests, primarily in Eurasia. With a wingspan of 74 inches and a total length of 30 inches for females (males are slightly smaller), the eagle-owl is the largest species of owl. The eagle-owl has distinctive ear tufts and orange eyes. It has a buff underbelly that is streaked with darker color.

Mostly found in mountainous regions or coniferous forests, the eagle-owl is a nocturnal predator that preys on small mammals, reptiles, amphibians, fish, large insects and earthworms. Eagle-owls prefer a concealed location for breeding, such as gullies or among rocks. They lay up to six eggs in the nest at intervals that hatch at different times. After the eggs are laid, the female incubates the eggs and broods the young while the male provides for her her and for the nestlings. After all of the eggs have hatched, parental care is continued for another five months.

The Eurasian eagle-owl has a number of vocalizations, including its song, which can be heard at great distances. It is a deep *ooh-hu*; the male emphasizes the first syllable, whereas females have a more high-pitched *uh-hu* song. In close quarters, eagle-owls express annoyance with bill-clicking and cat-like spitting, sometimes taking on a defensive posture: lowered head, ruffled back feathers, fanned tail, and spread wings.

Healthy adults have no natural predators, which makes them an apex predator, though they can be mobbed by smaller birds such as hawks or other owls. The leading cause of death, however, are man-made: electrocution, traffic accidents, and shooting. The eagle-owl can live up to 20 years in the wild; in captivity, without having to face difficult natural conditions, they can live much longer, with reports of up to 60 years in zoo settings. The Eurasian eagle-owl has a habitat that ranges 12 million square miles across Europe and Asia, and its population is estimated between 250,000 and 2.5 million individuals, landing it in the IUCN's "least concern" category. They can usually be found in large numbers in areas hardly populated by humans;

however, eagle-owls have been observed living on farmland or in park-like settings in European cities.

The cover image is from the *Braukhaus Lexicon*. The cover fonts are URW Typewriter and Guardian Sans. The text font is Adobe Minion Pro; the heading font is Adobe Myriad Condensed; and the code font is Dalton Maag's Ubuntu Mono.

Have it your way.

Get even more for your money.

Join the O'Reilly Community, and register the O'Reilly books you own. It's free, and you'll get:

- $4.99 ebook upgrade offer
- 40% upgrade offer on O'Reilly print books
- Membership discounts on books and events
- Free lifetime updates to ebooks and videos
- Multiple ebook formats, DRM FREE
- Participation in the O'Reilly community
- Newsletters
- Account management
- 100% Satisfaction Guarantee

Signing up is easy:

1. Go to: oreilly.com/go/register
2. Create an O'Reilly login.
3. Provide your address.
4. Register your books.

Note: English-language books only

To order books online:
oreilly.com/store

For questions about products or an order:
orders@oreilly.com

To sign up to get topic-specific email announcements and/or news about upcoming books, conferences, special offers, and new technologies:
elists@oreilly.com

For technical questions about book content:
booktech@oreilly.com

To submit new book proposals to our editors:
proposals@oreilly.com

O'Reilly books are available in multiple DRM-free ebook formats. For more information:
oreilly.com/ebooks